MW00582958

The Tug Is the Drug

37 Fly-Fishing Essays from the New York Times *& Beyond*

Chris Santella

STACKPOLE
BOOKS

Guilford, Connecticut
Blue Ridge Summit, Pennsylvania

STACKPOLE BOOKS
An imprint of Globe Pequot, the trade division of
The Rowman & Littlefield Publishing Group, Inc.
4501 Forbes Blvd., Ste. 200
Lanham, MD 20706
www.rowman.com

Distributed by NATIONAL BOOK NETWORK

First published as an e-book in 2014 by Headwater Books/Midcurrent
First Stackpole Books hardcover edition, 2017
First Stackpole Books paperback edition, 2022

British Library Cataloguing in Publication Information available

Library of Congress Cataloging-in-Publication Data

Names: Santella, Chris, author.
Title: The tug is the drug : 37 fly-fishing essays from the New York times & beyond / Chris Santella.
Description: First Stackpole Books hardcover edition. | Guilford, Connecticut: Stackpole Books, 2017. | "First published as an e-book in 2014 by Headwater Books/Midcurrent." | Includes bibliographical references and index.
Identifiers: LCCN 2016039876 (print) | LCCN 2016043151 (ebook) | ISBN 9780811719636 (hardback : alk. paper) | ISBN 9780811771290 (pbk : alk. paper) Subjects: LCSH: Fly fishing—Anecdotes.
Classification: LCC SH456 .S245 2017 (print) | LCC SH456 (ebook) | DDC 799.12/4—dc23
LC record available at https://lccn.loc.gov/2016039876

∞™ The paper used in this publication meets the minimum requirements of American National Standard for Information Sciences—Permanence of Paper for Printed Library Materials, ANSI/NISO Z39.48-1992.

The following essays first appeared in the *New York Times*: "When the Roosterfish Start to Run, Anglers Just Try to Keep Up," "Calgary—A City Where Trout Fishing Does Not Go to Die," "A Ferocious Gift Lures Anglers to Christmas Island," "Chasing Juvenile Tarpon through Yucatán Mangroves," "Off the Links, Onto the Stream," "Once Considered 'Trash,' Carp Become Worthy Fly Rod Target," "Seeking Stripers in the Shallows of Maine's Casco Bay," "In Ireland, Fishing for Salmon That Like a Crowd," "On Our Own on Alaska's Kanektok River," "Casting with the Master," "Salmonflies Awaken Western Trout, Anglers," "The Fish Whose Bite Is as Fierce as its Name," "White Nights of Salmon," "Fly Anglers Are Drawn to a Toothy Adversary," "The Addictive Allure of the Steelhead's Tug," "Lobstermen Turn to Guiding in the Yucatán," "Makos on the Fly," "Size *Does* Matter When Spey Casting," and "The Man Who Brought Trout to a Valley of Gravel."

"The Karma of Broken Trailers," "Nato and the Human Anchor," "How to Get Skunked on the Bulkley and Threaten Your Marriage at the Same Time," "No Good Deed Goes Unpunished," and "Feed Your Fish Head" first appeared in *The Flyfish Journal*.

"Postcard from Homosassa," "Mojitos, Muchachas, y Sábalo," "The Rainbows of Crater Lake," and "It Was *Epic, Dude*!" first appeared in *Fly Rod & Reel*; "The Greedy Beady Egg Man," "Dylan: The Fly-Fishing Years," and "Smallmouth in Greater Portland" in *The Drake*; "Fishing with Lewis & Clark" in *Portland Magazine*; "Frank Moore, Dean of the North Umpqua," and "Rainbows All" in *Trout*; "Traveling Light" in *Atlantic Salmon Journal*; "Among the Hobbit Trout" in the *Washington Post*; and "The Pledge" in *Gray's Sporting Journal*.

Contents

Acknowledgments

I've had the good fortune over the last thirty years to make many fine fishing friends who have furthered my horizons, both in terms of angling experiences and a greater appreciation of life. This list includes Howard Kyser, Peter Marra, Ken Matsumoto, Jeff Sang, Joe Runyon, Mark Harrison, Peter Gyerko, Tim Purvis, Geoff Roach, Kenton Quist, Tom Bodkin, Mike Ishida, Mike Marcus, Kevin Wright, John Smith, David Moscowitz, Ken Helm, Bryce Tedford, Darrell Hanks, Hamp Byerly, Chris Conaty, Steve Cook. Mark Tegen, Allen Sing, Dinty Leach, and Mac McKeever. (Keep it in neutral, Mac!) I look forward to many more days on the water with these friends and friends to come. I wish to thank Jay Nichols and Marshall Cutchin for initially seeing the possibilities of this project, and the fine editors who recognized some worth in these stories in the first place—Jason Stallman and Tom Connelly at the *New York Times*, Kirk Deeter at *Trout*, Greg Thomas at *Fly Rod & Reel*, Steve Duda at *The Flyfish Journal*, among others. I also extend kudos to Sloan Morris, Keith Carlson, and Doug Mateer, who've helped put fly fishing to music in our band, Catch & Release. Finally, I want to extend a special thanks to my wife, Deidre, and my daughters, Cassidy and Annabel, who've humored my absence on far too many occasions so I could pursue my favorite pastime . . . and to my parents, who are not anglers, but always encouraged me to chase after my passions.

A Ferocious Gift Lures Anglers to Christmas Island

As a non–fish eater, I was taken aback when Peter Kairaoi, lead guide for Christmas Island Outfitters, took a healthy bite from a dead and rather pungent milkfish he was shredding and tossing into the water for chum. My gag reflex was preempted by a burst of adrenaline as Kairaoi interrupted his sashimi snack to yell "Trevally!" A large shadow moved onto the flat, zigging and zagging in search of its next meal. It sped toward us in the shallows until half of its immense head was above the water. I cast my 12-weight—a telephone pole of a rod—in the fish's direction, hoping that my offering would prove tempting, or at least discourage its advance.

Giant trevally are a little bit scary.

Giant trevally (GTs) are the largest of the 33 species of trevally that swim in the Pacific and Indian Oceans. Silver shaded with prominently forked tails, they are easily distinguished from other trevally species by their steep head profile. GTs will prey on anything they can catch and squeeze into their capacious mouth—mullet, juvenile milkfish, even bonefish. Generally found in deeper water, they will sweep onto the flats—often in groups of three, four, or five fish—in pursuit of prey. Giant trevally can reach weights of 120 pounds and more, though anglers are more likely to encounter specimens in the 10- to 50-pound range. Many are thankful for that.

"Anyone who has had the opportunity to fish for giant trevally knows that if you get an opportunity at a trophy GT—a fish of 50 pounds or better—many things need to go right to get the fish to hand," said Brian

Gies, co-owner of Fly Water Travel. "More often than not, somewhere in the string of events something goes wrong—a rod breaks, knots give way, or a coral head severs the line—and you're left standing on the flat, heart and mind racing, knees weak, playing the situation back in your mind."

It was the promise of bonefish that initially lured anglers to Christmas Island, an isolated coral atoll some 1,200 miles south of Honolulu, part of the island nation of Kiribati. Since the early 1980s, the atoll's vast interior lagoon—a mix of sand and coral flats interspersed with deep cuts that usher tidal water to and fro—has been renowned as one of the world's most prolific and reliable venues for the sleek, finicky sport fish. In the course of stalking bonefish, anglers discovered GTs—sometimes in hot pursuit of the bonefish they attempted to play to hand!

There are three ways that fly anglers can pursue giant trevally on Christmas Island. One can establish a post on a flat adjacent to channels with a healthy current and chum, waiting for the fish parts to draw in other baitfish that will (hopefully) in turn lure in the GTs; one can slowly cruise the edges of the flats in one of the island's motorized catamarans, scanning for GTs that can then be stalked on foot; or, one can pursue bonefish on the flats while carrying a 12-weight rod in your pack, and switch rods if you happen upon ambushing GTs (easier said than done).

Chumming proved most productive for my group, though it was not until the fifth day of fishing that our flies found purchase. After capturing a brace of milkfish in a seine net, guides Moana Kofe and T. John anchored our cat on a small coral island and positioned four anglers opposite a channel. Darkening hues of turquoise hinted at the deepening water before us—the domain of trevally. As Kofe and John tossed chunks of milkfish into the water, great frigatebirds hovered just above them, occasionally plucking a morsel from the surface. GTs materialized in less than 10 minutes—two fish at the point of the island, a gang of four in the shallows in front of the channel. They moved deliberately in search of food, churning the water and swirling at our flies. Two anglers hooked up in rapid succession; one had only six feet of leader outside of his rod tip when the fish took. Soon we had all hooked and landed fish from the melee, the largest approaching 40 pounds.

Before the fishing slowed, I flipped my streamer, a concoction of long white chicken feathers, to the edge of a group of circling trevally. A leviathan—Kofe estimated it at near 60 pounds—charged out of the depths, seizing the fly on the run. Though my drag was tightened to maximum tension, the fish peeled line and backing off as though I were using a toy reel. The fish raced toward the channel at the far end of the island, and I chased after it, dodging under the lines of my fellow anglers in an attempt to keep the leader and fly line high and away from coral heads. After 75 yards, I could go no further. My rod pulsed as the reel gave up line—100, 150, then 200 yards. For a moment, I entertained the vision of my rod shattering under this immense pressure, shards of splintering graphite piercing my carotid artery. I would perish by trevally on this lonely coral isle! There was nothing I could do but hope that the fish would stop and let me regain some line. Then there was simply nothing.

I reeled in several football fields of backing to learn that my 100-pound leader had been sliced.

At least I had not lost my fly line, too.

The Karma of Broken Trailers

Every generation or so, the subject of paving the Deschutes River access road from Sherars Falls to Mack's Canyon is brought up for discussion. The notion is always quickly shot down, with the guide community leading the charge. "The crowds will be unbearable on an already crowded river," is the sentiment. Prospects for a paved road are tabled for another 10 or 20 years, and some of its opponents proceed to drive the roughly 17-mile stretch at twice the posted speed limit—especially during the steelhead season—leaving the already marginal gravel road a washboard hell.

One that can be very hard on trailers.

I own a one-third share of a drift boat, and consequently am sometimes asked to donate a trip for a school auction or assist friends with overflow guests. One weekend last September, I was slated for two such trips, back-to-back, both floating from the Beavertail campground to Mack's. Prior to the adventure, I had my tires rotated and checked, knowing the travails that waited. I picked up the boat from my friend's driveway and proceeded to Maupin.

At 4:30 the next morning, my friend (and his sturdy Tacoma Supercab) began the drive north to Beavertail. When we left the paved road at Sherars, my Subaru was engulfed in his dust; but soon his taillights were out of sight. That's because I drive *very slow* on the access road, hoping to get my rig down and back in one piece. There was a blush of pink above the rimrock as I descended from the road to Beavertail. Reaching the bottom, I could see my friends at the put-in, wadered up and waiting. I circled the campground and rounded the final bend to approach the put-in. As my wheels straightened, there was an abrupt thud. I stopped, expecting I'd hung up on a rogue rock or popped one of my recently rotated tires. My eyes drifted to my passenger-side mirror. There, I spied one of my trailer tires rolling toward some brush. Its slow revolutions, with a woozy wobble and finally a dramatic leftward flop, had a cartoon quality about it. I found myself snickering, even though I sensed that the parting of the wheel from the trailer's axle had ended my fishing day, and would likely pose other hardships.

I turned off the car, rolled the wheel from the brush back to the trailer, and looked at the axle. I'm not mechanically inclined, but even a cursory glance in the half light of the canyon made it quite apparent that I'd be needing professional assistance. The hub was gone, and the odds of finding it somewhere between here and Sherars seemed less than low. I walked to the put-in to alert my party that they'd be going it alone and returned to the trailer. For a good 10 minutes, I stared at the axle, hoping that I could reattach the wheel through some force of will. This failed. My friends waved as they floated downstream.

It was 5:30 a.m.

There's no cell reception to speak of at the Beavertail launch, and I'd be adding insult to injury if I got stuck with a shuttle fee for a shuttle that would not happen. So I detached my crippled trailer and drove back up to the access road. A few miles toward Maupin, I found coverage and left my shuttle driver a message. Part of me wanted to keep driving and leave the trailer to heal itself.

I was back at the trailer by 6:15.

Some campers in Beavertail were beginning to stir, but lacking a flatbed, I doubted that they could offer much more than sympathy. Then I recalled that Beavertail had a camp host—and the camp host, Chris, was the wife of a steelhead guide I knew. As I approached the camp, Hawkeye (the guide) was making coffee; he had just come off a trip from Mack's to the Mouth. He fixed me a cup and I explained my quandary. "Chris will call Barnett's for you when she wakes up," Hawkeye said with a reassuring grin. "This isn't the first time a trailer has gone bust down here." Another cup of coffee and Chris was up. Soon she was walking around the campground with an antenna-like apparatus affixed to her cell phone to get coverage. She was smiling when she returned. "George has one emergency to take care of, but he will be down in about three hours," she reported.

Hawkeye put another pot of coffee on (and then another), heated up some pop 'n fresh cinnamon rolls, and we waited. We chatted about the current steelhead season (okay), the previous season (very good), and future seasons (hopeful). The cool of dawn gave way to the pleasant warmth of midmorning. After the fifth pot of coffee, the rumble of the flatbed could be heard. Soon the wounded trailer and its cargo was loaded on the flatbed. I extended Chris and Hawkeye a heartfelt thanks and followed George the 17-odd miles back to Maupin.

It was 11:15.

Back in Maupin, George assessed the situation. "Your wheel's okay, the axle is okay. You just need a new hub to hold everything on. I'm gonna have lunch, and then I'll get on it. Should be a few hours." That didn't seem too bad. I'd missed one trip, but maybe my second could be saved. I considered wadering up and finding a run to fish, but didn't want to be absent if George needed me. And the sun was high anyway. I made myself a sandwich, resisted the temptation to break into the beers I'd brought for my guests, and parked myself on the steps of the public library adjacent to George's shop and perused a copy of *The New Yorker*, which I'd thrown in the car. There was a particularly good story by John McPhee on the British Open golf tourney. One hour passed, then two. I didn't want to seem pushy, but I was beginning to become concerned about my auction trip the following day—would I have a trailer? I meekly approached George in the back. "How are we looking?" I asked. "Oh, my wife had to pick up a part in The Dalles," George replied. "She'll be back in an hour or so. I forgot tell you. Sorry."

As the sun made its way west, I moved across the street to a set of benches outside the Redside Tavern, downtown Maupin's premier (and only) watering hole. Believing, again, that my trailer situation would not become better with beer, I abstained. Three guys on Harleys pulled up and waddled into the bar. They seemed like wannabe bikers; their helmets and panniers were decorated with tasteful stickers like "Thanks, Virgins—for NOTHING!" and "Save a Mouse—Eat a Pussy!"

Several more hours passed. I read the McPhee article a second time.

At 5:15, George motioned me over. The trailer was done. I called my auction guest in Portland and told her all systems were go, reunited with my trailer and drift boat, and rolled back down the hill to my evening's lodging. It had been an arduous day, marked by long hours of waiting and brief crises of faith. Not unlike steelhead fishing. Though I could've easily parked the trailer, popped a beer, and called it an early night, I knew the sun was dipping below the rimrock, and decided that the last hour of daylight may as well be enjoyed on the river.

I'm not a religious person, but I do vaguely believe in karma—or at least the notion that one's good or bad actions eventually come home to roost. I had not performed any great acts of charity, courage, or selflessness that Friday, but given the problems I'd faced, I'd behaved with a certain level of decorum. I hadn't sworn (much) or kicked the trailer when the wheel departed. I'd been patient in Chris and Hawkeye's camp, and perhaps even more patient on the library steps in Maupin. I had resisted the default urge to drown my disappointments, had kept my promise to the following day's guests, and had opted to persevere and visit the river instead of accepting the easy defeat of sitting my lazy butt on the porch of my rented cabin.

For these reasons, I was rewarded with a steelhead, even though another angler had just left the run I fished . . . and that I cast for only 15 minutes. As it was a hatchery buck, I conked it on the head, walked up to the access road, and handed it to the first passerby who stopped.

I want my trailer karma to keep circling back.

Traveling Light

On the Ponoi, sometimes a fresh change of underwear is all you need.

HELSINKI AIRPORT—THE JET LAG (13 HOURS IN THE AIR AND A major time zone swap) may have explained my calm indifference when after 15 minutes, my green Hawaiian-print duffel bag—holding all my clothing and fishing gear for a long-anticipated Ponoi adventure—had yet to appear. Marjaliisa, the Frontiers International Travel representative on the ground in Helsinki, was a comforting presence. "This is not the first time bags have been misplaced," she reassured me with a knowing smile. "There are two more flights coming in today from Amsterdam. There's no reason to be concerned." Marjaliisa escorted me to the KLM baggage desk, where a representative in a crisp KLM uniform filled out the requisite paperwork.

Later that afternoon I laid my head on a fluffy down pillow in downtown Helsinki's tasteful Hotel Kamp for a nap. Reveries of plentiful salmon mixed with a sense of relief that I would soon be exchanging my travel-weary togs for a fresher suit of clothes.

FIVE A.M., HOTEL KAMP—At the breakfast buffet that is arranged by the hotel exclusively for departing anglers, I filled my plate with scrambled eggs and joined my traveling partner, Kirk, and another Ponoi-bound angler named Ian. Kirk, who had traveled from the States on KLM, was also without his luggage. Ian was recounting a tale from his first trip to the Ponoi. "There were two Irishmen whose luggage had been lost en route to Murmansk," Ian said. "They showed up at the Ryabaga

Camp with the clothes on their backs. The camp manager and the guides pooled together some gear so the Irishmen could fish. On the last night, one of the Irishmen got up and made a long toast, thanking the camp for all they had done." I smiled and nodded as Ian finished his story. Admittedly, I was more focused on my eggs, as I knew that Marjaliisa was on the case. The eggs seemed lighter than the scrambled eggs at home. "Perhaps they use reindeer milk," I pondered to myself.

A small bus spirited us through Helsinki as late-night revelers weaved along the sidewalk toward home in the already bright sunlight. When we reached the airport, Marjaliisa appeared considerably less buoyant. "They're not here," she said. She did not strike me as having a wild sense of humor, so I was fairly certain this was not a joke. After chuckling nervously and staring at my feet for five minutes, the reality of my situation struck. There was no time for the five stages of grief. The flight to Murmansk was leaving in less than an hour. I had better spring into action.

After quickly clearing security (one advantage of traveling light), Kirk and I tried to locate an outdoor clothing store. I was hopeful—after all, there are Columbia and Ex Officio stores in the Portland and Seattle airports—but the duty-free shop in Helsinki was lacking in sportswear—or any clothing, for that matter. But they did stock lots of single malt scotch, and Kirk wisely secured a large bottle. Working our way toward the gate for Murmansk, we passed an electronics store, a gift shop, and a boutique of sorts that carried some men's clothing, including socks, golf shirts, and underwear. I picked up a three-pack of briefs. When I saw the price—35 euros (approximately US$50)—the frugal Yankee in me balked. Seventeen dollars for a pair of underwear? I put the three-pack down, reasoning that better deals could be found in Murmansk. A mental flash of pre-Perestroika newsreels showing Muscovites lining up around the block to buy toilet paper disabused me of this feverish dream of Murmansk department stores, and I fetched the underwear. A two-for-one special made the 35 euros a little easier to bear.

And, they were Calvin Kleins.

My instincts about the shopping opportunities (or lack thereof) available in the Murmansk airport were correct, though the waiting room had obviously been upgraded since a friend of mine had passed through five years before. The uncomfortable furniture and poor air circulation had been maintained, but now bar service was available. *Na Zdorov'ye!* Soon we boarded the Mi-8 helicopter that would spirit us south to the river. I nestled into my spot along the long bench seat on the left side of the helicopter, taking some comfort in the thought that the absence of my bag provided a tiny bit of extra legroom for my fellow passengers . . . though even a business class seat would not quite have compensated for the noise and the gas fumes of the Mi-8.

RYABAGA CAMP, Ponoi River—True to her parting words at the Helsinki airport, Marjaliisa had emailed ahead to the American manager, Matt Breuer, concerning our plight. Within minutes of walking down Ryabaga's self-proclaimed "Stairway to Heaven," Oliver, a young first-year Ponoi guide from England, appeared at my tent cabin with a pair of waders and wading shoes. Not long after, Owen, another first-year guide from the States, arrived with a pair of fleece pants, a T-shirt, two pairs of socks, a fleece jacket, and a rain shell. With the spey rod that Matt brought over in the morning and a few tube flies purchased from Ryabaga's little fly shop—German Shneldas and Max's Ponoi Nails, among them—I was outfitted for action.

And action there was, beyond my wildest expectations. During the week of my late-May visit, anglers averaged over 60 fish to hand. Several anglers had 30-fish days, and released well over 100 fish over six days of fishing. (Catch-and-release is strictly practiced on the Ponoi.) Granted, a large percentage of the fish were grilse in the five- to seven-pound class, and some of the MWS salmon were not exactly nickel bright.

But more than 60 Atlantic salmon to hand—including a good number on skated flies (a small tube on a hook was as effective as anything)—is a number that will likely eclipse the number of salmon I'll catch in the rest of my lifetime . . . unless I make it back to the Ponoi. Grilse or not, I was ecstatic.

If a bit aromatic.

It was a challenge to remain presentable for mealtimes with my modest wardrobe. I showered frequently, especially given the unseasonably warm weather our group encountered. I set my fleece pants in the early evening sunlight to air out. Matt's team laundered my travel ensemble midweek, giving it a new lease on life. A dram or two of Kirk's single malt as we revisited the day in his tent cabin made my person more bearable . . . at least to myself.

I had the undergarment part of the equation under control.

On our last evening in camp, Matt read off the week's catch statistics (the second highest on record, for those counting) and congratulated the high rods. As the applause subsided, I stood up, still grimacing slightly from the obligatory vodka shot that follows applause in these parts, and prepared to toast Matt and his team for so graciously provisioning Kirk and me in the absence of our bags. Remembering the Irishman that had come several years before me, I paused, reaching deep for a level of eloquence befitting the solemnity of the occasion. Perhaps it was the vodka working its magic, but instead of summoning Yeats or Joyce, my thoughts raced to a series of mildly scandalous commercials from the early 1990s. In each of the spots, models in various stages of undress pouted and stretched before concluding that nothing could come between them and their Calvins.

Had I been faster on my feet, I might have parlayed this strange flashback into something clever: "Were it not for the generosity of the Ponoi River staff, I would've been releasing salmon all week in nothing but my Calvins . . . not a sight I would wish upon any of you!" Instead, I mumbled "Thanks for everything" or something equally innocuous.

The following day I was reunited with my duffel bag, which had been waiting patiently under the careful watch of the bellhop at the Hotel Kamp. I was tempted to inspect the two fly boxes and the three rods and four reels that had been waylaid 500 miles short of their ultimate destination. But there was little time and many miles ahead so instead I opened a side pocket to cram in what little luggage I had brought with me from the Ponoi.

It was a tight fit, but I was able to squeeze my new Calvins in.

Calgary—A City Where Trout Fishing Does Not Go to Die

Alberta's Bow River flows 387 miles in a southeasterly direction from its headwaters at Bow Glacier, north of Lake Louise in Banff National Park. In its upper reaches, the Bow has all the trappings of a classic alpine trout stream—conifer-lined banks, gravelly riffles, sweeping backdrops of vertiginous mountains, and a slightly off-color tint that suggests cover for lunkers lurking just below the surface. But appearances can be deceiving. While the upper Bow does hold trout, its icy, glacial-fed waters do not sustain fish in large numbers.

Driving east from Banff, the Canadian Rockies give way to rolling hills and then prairie. Not long after leaving the mountains, the western edges of Calgary begin to come into view. Once a quiet city on the edge of the plains with once-a-year notoriety for the world's largest rodeo, Calgary has nearly tripled in size in the last 40 years to over a million residents; this, thanks to an oil boom, a winter Olympics hosting coup (in 1988), and the increasing appeal of an outdoors-oriented lifestyle that a city like Calgary offers. The Bow River bifurcates Calgary as it rolls towards its junction with the South Saskatchewan River, ultimately reaching Hudson Bay. Generally speaking, the demands and detritus of a budding metropolis spell the death (or at least considerable degradation) of a trout stream. But in the case of the Bow, Calgary's swelling population—and more specifically, its wastewater treatment needs—have helped create a world-class fishery in the 30-odd miles of river from the city east to the rural town of Carseland. Here, wild rainbow and brown trout *average* nearly 18 inches in length, and browns stretching over 25 inches are regularly encountered.

In Calgary it's not inconceivable to hook the trout of a lifetime during your lunch break and be back at the office in time to lead the 2 p.m. work-in-progress update meeting.

It is the infusion of nutrients into the Bow's clean, cold water from Calgary's two wastewater treatment plants—Fish Creek and Bonnybrook—that is most responsible for elevating the river to blue-ribbon status. The inflow—from car wash leftovers to bathroom water—goes through a four-stage treatment process. The effluent that's released back into the river is quite clean, though it has just enough phosphorous and nitrogen to foster an incredibly rich aquatic ecosystem. Wastewater spurs plant growth, which encourages insect growth, which in turn feeds trout. "The Bow River fishery has grown and improved as the city has grown," said Brian Meagher, a Provincial Biologist with Trout Unlimited Canada who works in Calgary. "Residents have come to recognize what we have here, and the fishery has evolved as people have become more conscious of the river and how their actions can impact it."

The brown and rainbow trout that call the Bow home are not native to the river. Both were introduced in the 1920s; the browns reached the river when a truck carrying 45,000 fingerling broke down near the river before reaching its intended destination, and the driver released them into the Bow, rather than see them perish. The success of these introduced species has had its downside. Native westslope cutthroat trout and bull trout have been significantly marginalized in the lower river, though their populations are more stable to the west.

How the trout of the Bow came to be there and how they grew to such gargantuan proportions was far from our minds as my fishing partner, Ken Matsumoto, and I careened toward the boat put-in at McKinnon Flats. We just hoped to find a few. "The fishing in town can be quite good, especially for the browns," our guide, Jason Eggleton of Country Pleasures Fly Fishing, said as we strung up our 5-weights. "But when it's off, it's definitely off, and the last few days' reports haven't been good. Today, we're going to float about 15 miles of what tends to be the most productive stretch." The Bow at this point is a large river, from 100 yards across to nearly twice that size. Jason instructed us to tie on foam grasshopper patterns, as these juicy terrestrials were beginning to appear with the August heat. Our large flies were also similar to the golden stoneflies that had gotten the trout's attention in July. Once such large bugs imprint on the trout's memory, they'll continue to take imitations even after the real insects are gone. (The Bow's hatches can be quite prolific, and anglers can expect to encounter pale morning duns, tricos, caddis, and blue-winged olives, depending on the season.)

On this particular day, the fish were atypically disinterested in our offerings. Jason drifted the boat 60-odd feet from the shoreline—a mix of farmland and stands of pines and hardwood—instructing us to cast as close to the reeds as we could, and to drop the fly in pockets of slightly faster-moving water whenever possible. "They'll rest in as little as six inches of water," he said. I was incredulous until a stroll along the bank later in the day proved this declaration true. I tried to position myself to make a cast without spooking the 20-plus-inch rainbow Jason had spotted finning in the shallows, and promptly found a tree with my backcast. The fish moved slowly off toward deeper water before I could re-rig.

As the sun began to fade in the west, we heard a loud splashing downstream as we cast to a trout taking small caddisflies in a back eddy. I looked over, expecting to see one of those legendary 30-inch Bow River browns aggressively feeding. Instead, there was a moose calf struggling to crawl up the bank as its mother looked on.

Chasing Juvenile Tarpon through Yucatán Mangroves

I can't help but think of *Heart of Darkness* as guide Carlos Castillo from Costa Maya Lodge pushes my companion, Geoff Roach, and me through a tunnel in the mangrove swamps that envelop much of Costa Maya—the inland region of the southern Yucatán stretching from Bahia Espiritu Santo in the north and Belize in the south. The unrelenting sun is momentarily blotted out, and egrets, herons, and other birds I can't quite identify scream hysterically as we negotiate our way around a sunken panga boat blown here from the sea by Hurricane Dean in 2007. Mangrove crabs scuttle above my fingers as I grab branches to pull our flats boat through a channel that's barely wide enough to accommodate the craft. After several twists and turns, there's a flash of blue at the end of our mangrove maze, and the crash of a heavy body dropping into water.

We've arrived at Murky, one of Costa Maya's saltwater lakes, where lucky anglers have the privilege to do battle with "baby" tarpon ranging from six to 40 pounds . . . and more.

The mangrove-enshrouded lakes and their inhabitants—snook, barracuda, and snapper, in addition to the tarpon—are phenomena peculiar to the state of Quintana Roo on the eastern side of the Yucatán Peninsula. Here, *cenotes* (pronounced "say-no-tays") punctuate the limestone strata, granting access to underground rivers and caverns. Near the town of Majahual, cenotes connect roughly a dozen lakes to the Caribbean, allowing salt water (and a host of its denizens) to pass freely back and forth. The lakes themselves are shallow, seldom exceeding depths of four to six feet; devoid of predators and brimming with baitfish and other feed, they provide an ideal nursery ground for young tarpon. The Mayan people revered cenotes, viewing them as portals to a spiritual world below the earth. Fly anglers who've had the chance to visit the lakes profess a similar reverence. The reason is simple—the tarpon here are contained in a relatively finite space, providing visitors multiple opportunities to jump fish. Since access is limited to a small group of permit holders, the fish see very few flies, and thus remain aggressive.

Aggressive may be a gross understatement. While these juvenile tarpon are a fraction of the size of the hundred-plus-pound behemoths that patrol the flats and reefs of the Caribbean, they lack none of their elders' penchant for violent takes, which telegraph through an 8-weight fly rod like a roundhouse right to the temple. If you're not jolted into the present by the tarpon's take, their first jump—within one to three seconds of the take, in my experience—will put you in a panic mode. The visceral fury of that leap, with the sun glinting off the fish's large silver scales as if it were a spiraling chrome bumper instead of the largest member of the herring family, sparks an unfortunate Pavlovian response from unschooled tarpon anglers: you immediately lift the rod, which 99 percent of the time will terminate your connection to the tarpon. (First-timers will claim that they're reverting to trout-fishing techniques; I believe the rod lifting is a fear response, an attempt on the angler's part to shield his or herself from the projectile outside the boat!)

Fly fishing for tarpon on the cenote-fed lakes around Majahual is something of an endurance contest. While Geoff and I cast to many tarpon that we or Carlos spotted, a majority of the day we traded off making long, blind casts with large flies to the mangrove shoreline, sometimes battling a significant wind. The closer your fly is to the mangroves the better, as the fish often tuck far beneath the foliage; it was not uncommon to hear single or multiple fish splashing about in a foot of water under the mangroves. (On one occasion we heard an extended period of crashing accompanied by the agitated cries of egrets, followed by silence. "*Cocodrilo*," Carlos said matter of factly.) Casts to the edge or below the mangroves would occasionally draw a fish out from the shadows, but more often we'd overshoot the mark and have to pole to the shoreline to retrieve our popper, Clouser, or Snookeroo, a floating deer hair creation resembling a steroidal Muddler Minnow that's a favorite on the lakes. "You're fishing for *mono* [monkey]," Carlos would say with a smile. Sometimes, a tarpon or snook would lazily swim past as we untangled the fly, adding insult to injury.

When the angler manages to avoid the mangroves and get the fly in front of the fish, it's important to keep your fly moving. "If the fish gets too close, it will smell the fly and realize it's not something to eat," Carlos explained. Fish will follow for long distances, sometimes exploding on the fly within a rod's length of the boat.

On the afternoon of our last day on the tarpon lakes, I'd been able to jump several fish, lifting my rod each time to cut my battle short. As Geoff climbed to the casting station, a fish swam into view between the boat and the mangroves. Geoff made a quick, short cast and the fish quickly obliged. With admirable composure, Geoff kept his rod tip down, strip-set the hook in the tarpon's hard jaw, and braced for the tarpon's leap. When it soared skyward, he dutifully bowed the rod, minimizing the slack line that allows the fish to frequently throw the hook. The fish stood its ground, neither ripping line from the reel nor surrendering to the pressure of Geoff's rod. A few minutes later, the standoff was over, and a fish approaching 20 pounds was in the boat. As Geoff removed the fly and returned the fish to Murky, a tiger heron cried out in seeming appreciation from atop the mangroves, its hoarse cry rising above the crash of the Caribbean surf 100 yards to the east.

Off the Links, Onto the Stream

While shepherds were whacking bits of dried sheep dung around the spongy coastline of eastern Scotland in golf's formative days, in the late 15th century, sportsmen and women to the south in England were tinkering with the use of artificial baits in what would come to be known as fly fishing.

The two sports share more than their ancestry. Both tend to appeal to those with contemplative, even analytic, temperaments. Both can arouse a powerful, even obsessive, fascination among the faithful, as well as a never-ending accumulation of gear.

The connection between golf and fly fishing first struck me 10 years ago, when a fishing guide recounted a day when he had taken Tiger Woods and Mark O'Meara out on the Deschutes River in Oregon to cast flies for steelhead. As my friend recalled this special day on the river, I noted that many golfers I know fly fish, and vice versa. Perhaps it's the outdoor setting, pitting man against an indifferent if not inimical nature, be it in the form of finicky trout or gaping bunkers. Perhaps it's the similarity of the motions of swinging and casting—the fact that the ball or fly goes farther when you move smoothly.

"There's never a locker room on tour that doesn't have a fly rod in there," said Davis Love III, a 20-time winner on the PGA Tour and the captain of the American Ryder Cup team. "Some of the guys will bring rods around with them on their practice rounds to make a few casts."

Love said it was the lakes on golf courses that got him interested in fishing. He began dabbling in fly fishing because several other players on the PGA Tour, especially O'Meara, Jack Nicklaus, and Paul Azinger, enjoyed it.

Love has fished in places like the Bahamas and Silver Creek, in Idaho, but his current favorite fishing spot on the tour is the Blue Monster at Doral, near Miami. "One of the ponds on the Blue Monster course has peacock bass," he said. "You can see them hanging around the rocks way out. Sometimes a group of us will go out after the day's round. You have to make your longest cast."

For Nick Faldo, golf and fly fishing are intimately connected. He said he became interested in fishing in 1986 when he was changing his swing. "My doctor took me down to the River Test in the south of England to give me a break from the range," Faldo said. "There's a famous mayfly hatch that occurs on the Test at that time, known as Duffers Fortnight. If you can't catch a fish then, you'll never catch one. I was hooked. I find fly fishing completely engrossing. I love the tranquility, the sound of the river. When you come upon a rising trout that's picky and you have to try six different fly patterns to get him to take, 30 or 40 minutes will fly by, and that fish has had your complete attention. When you're fishing, you're not clock watching. You get lost in time.

"Fly fishing is like golf in that you don't get a second chance, especially when casting to a bonefish. You quickly learn to get everything right—cast, line position, drag. One thing wrong, and 'bogey!'—you lose the fish."

Nick Price, winner of 18 tour events, including three majors, said one appeal of fly fishing for golfers was the way the fields of play changed and demanded different techniques. "Each golf course has its own kind of beauty, though a parkland layout is quite different from a links course," he said. "Likewise, a steelhead river in British Columbia is quite different than a chalkstream in England, though both have appeals. And both require different approaches to find success." Pro golfers, Price added, appreciate the solitude of fly fishing. "You can be playing in a major championship on Sunday, surrounded by throngs of people on the course, signing autographs before and after," Price said. "A day or two later, you can be alone on a bonefish flat in the Bahamas. The seclusion fly fishing provides is a nice balance."

Ben Crane, a four-time winner on the tour, described fly fishing as a "mental vacation" from the grind of the golf tour. "Playing on tour can be a little one-dimensional, as you're constantly on the road, thinking about one thing: golf," he said. But when he is fishing, Crane gets to think about something else. "When I'm out there, I think of only one thing for seven hours: what is the fish thinking?" he said. "You still have to be very focused. Where's the fish holding? What's the depth of the fly? Is it the right fly?

"In golf, saving one stroke a day can be huge; the difference between 72 and 71 can be $5 million. Likewise, in fly fishing, little details can mean catching more fish. Out on the course, golfers tend to go all-in. The best fly fishers also go all-in."

Frank Moore, Dean of the North Umpqua

THE FIRST THING YOU LEARN WHEN YOU MEET FRANK MOORE IS THAT he has a strong handshake. A bone-crushing, PSI-of-a-komodo dragon, champion cage-fighter kind of handshake.

It's not the handshake you'd expect from a nonagenarian of average build. And it's not a handshake that's intended to intimidate or establish some sort of alpha male dominance. When Frank Moore grabs your hand, he's making a connection and showing that he cares. He *really* cares.

There are a number of things that Frank cares dearly about. First and foremost, his wife of 70 years, Jeanne. Second, his family, which includes three adult children, seven grandchildren, and two great-grandchildren. And third, the North Umpqua River. No one can coax the North Umpqua's summer steelhead out of their elusive holding spots like Frank. And no one has done more to protect the river for the last half century.

Frank's love affair with the North Umpqua and its wild runs of steelhead began soon after he returned from Europe, where he was part of the Allied forces that stormed Utah Beach on D-Day. "I had seen the river once when I was a boy on a trip we took before my dad died in 1932," Frank recalled. "Even as a kid, I was taken with how beautiful it was. When Jeanne and I moved to Roseburg after the war, I'd be up on the river whenever I had a spare moment. The North Umpqua is an ethereal place, a little bit of heaven on earth; well, a lot of heaven! Over the years, the river has become part of me. I think of it a little like Eden after Adam and Eve's fall. Even though it's not as pristine as it used to be, it's still a great place."

Most serious steelheaders would agree that the North Umpqua is indeed a great place . . . among the best places. A river of astounding clarity and beauty, it flows west from its headwaters in Oregon's Cascade Range through mixed hardwood and pine forests to the town of Roseburg, where it joins with the river's south fork and flows onward to the Pacific. Each summer, thousands of wild steelhead return to the river; they'll spawn in the early winter in Steamboat Creek and other tributaries. Healthy winter runs of wild fish also spawn in the North Umpqua system, which hosts runs of Chinook and Coho salmon and sea-run cutthroat. Where some steelhead rivers are defined by long runs or riffle-pool structures, North Umpqua steelhead seem to revert to their early days as smolts, holding behind rocks, off ledges, and in a host of other unlikely spots. A road parallels the river for much of its course. Anglers can get an inkling of likely holding water by the presence of pullouts, though without some local knowledge, you'll most likely overlook them. I've wasted many an hour fishing a long run or pool, only to have Frank tell me later that fish never hold in that spot . . . but if I had cast out behind the rock in the fast water a quarter mile below the run in question, I *might* have found one.

I usually don't. But the experience of fishing the North Umpqua and visiting with Frank and Jeanne makes every trip worthwhile. "I think many consider the North Umpqua to be the finishing school for steelhead fly fishing," Frank offered. "Normally, you have to be a halfway-decent fly fisher to consistently hook a fish here. If you think you're good and want to improve, you can do so here on one of the most beautiful rivers around."

Most steelheaders I know take to the rivers of the Pacific Northwest with spey or switch rods. We need two-handed rods to make the long casts that are often required to cover the water. Frank's preferred weapon on the North Umpqua is a G. Loomis NRX, single-hand rod. He doesn't need a spey rod, as he can cast over 100 feet . . . and do so while perched on slippery-as-glass ledges amid heavy current and poking his backcasts through tiny holes in the foliage. Watching Frank fish is something to behold! The beauty of his performance with a fly rod has not gone unnoticed; Travel Oregon (the state's tourism arm) has featured him as part of its "Oregon Dreamer" campaign, and he's also been profiled on a popular public broadcasting program, *Oregon Field Guide*. Frank likes to fish an old-style Skunk pattern or a #8 Muddler Minnow. "I don't trim the deer hair on the Muddler head very much," he told me a few years back. "I call it an Ugly Muddler. Maybe it's the way the current teases the hairs, but who can tell? I think much of the time the angler is a lot more choosey than the fish. It's something to see them come up and take a free-floating fly or a skater. Sometimes, they'll just suck it under. Other times, they'll come three or four feet out of the air and take the fly coming down."

It wasn't long after moving to Roseburg that Frank's livelihood became enmeshed with the river. He explained:

> *In the late '40s, Clarence Gordon (who operated the North Umpqua Lodge) asked if I would like to guide for him. I hadn't been on the river long, but I was an adept angler, and could cover ground. I would literally run up and down the river in my waders to learn the pools and holding water. I was never sure if Clarence thought I'd make a good guide or merely wanted me with his clients so I would not be fishing the best pools for myself, but I began guiding. The lodge closed in 1951 (thanks in large part to the building of a dam upstream, which severely impacted water flows and caused severe siltation for several years). In 1957, Jeanne and I had the chance to buy the Forest Service lease from Clarence to operate the business on the site, which was then a store/gas station. We did it. At the same time we moved to Steamboat, one of the contractors who'd been working with his crew building the road (Highway 138) along the river up to Diamond Lake left his D-8 Cat at the store. He knew I could operate it, and he said that I could feel free to use it. I leveled off a spot in back of the store, above the river, and built a few cabins. That was the start of the Steamboat Inn.*

The Steamboat Inn has catered to anglers ever since. Its hearty breakfasts and fisherman's dinners have become an essential part of the North Umpqua experience for many visiting the river. Though Frank and Jeanne left the hospitality business in 1975, their home high above the river is still a nexus for steelheaders far and wide. (Nonfishers are welcome too.) Each of the many times I've visited the Moores, other well-wishers have stopped by to pay their respects. They'll usually be offered a cup of coffee. If the visitor is an angler, he or she may be invited out to Frank's trout pond to try a new rod or get a quick casting tip; if the visitor favors wildflowers, Jeanne will share stories of her latest finds (wildflowers are *her* passion). If you're under 70, Frank will call you "son" and mean it in the most fatherly way. And if you make a good roll cast on the pond, he'll exclaim, "That's it, son!" and give you a celebratory clap on the back that could easily send you into the pond if your legs aren't braced.

Generations of the North Umpqua's steelhead have learned to fear the sight of Frank Moore on the bank and the hypnotic appeal of one of his untrimmed Muddlers skittering across the surface. Yet the fish (and at least three generations of anglers) owe him some major props. A partial list of accomplishments on behalf of the river that he helped champion include: enacting significant changes to logging practices in the watershed to protect tributaries (this was facilitated by a film called *Pass Creek* made by advertising legend Hal Riney and his associate Dick Snider after Frank showed them what was happening in the upper watershed); the creation of a 31-mile fly-only section on the North Umpqua after Governor Tom McCall named him to the Oregon State Game Commission (The fly-only regs were put in place to protect the fish, not punish bait anglers; "The way fish stack up in the river, they were very vulnerable to bait anglers," Frank said.); and the banning of weighted flies in the fly-only section in the summer, as well as indicator nymphing (again, to protect the fish). Not all of his efforts have found success. "When the state decided that they were going to put hatchery steelhead in the North Umpqua, I initially thought it would be great," he remembered. "After the second return, I felt it was awful. The hatchery fish don't have the same body configuration as the natives. They're a mess, and most fight like an old boot. They're a different fish. I collared a biologist one day and told him, 'I bet you $1,000 I can tell a hatchery fish from a wild fish on the end of my line in five seconds.' He said he didn't have that kind of money. I suggested $100, then $1. Finally he said,

'The average person doesn't know the difference,' and that was that. His attitude was disappointing."

Though Frank is not the kind of man who courts attention, the world has noticed. He has received the National Wildlife Federation–Sears Roebuck Foundation Conservationist of the Year Award; the Izaak Walton League Beaver Award for conservation achievement; the Anders Award for wild trout management; the International Federation of Fly Fishing's (FFF) Conservation Award of the Year; and the Conservationist of the Year from the Wild Steelhead Coalition. He's also been enshrined in the World Fresh Water Fishing Hall of Fame.

One recognition that Frank Moore is especially proud of is his appointment as a Chevalier of the Legion of Honour, which was granted by President Nicolas Sarkozy in 2011 in recognition of France's appreciation for his contribution in the liberation of France during World War II. (He was also honored with a Luxembourg Medal of Honor, and was cited for Conspicuously Meritorious and Outstanding Performance of Military Duty while under Combat Conditions, by the U.S. Army, European Theater of Operations.) Amidst all the privations he endured at Utah Beach and beyond, the thought of fishing provided a level of comfort for Frank. "After we broke out of Normandy, my division (the U.S. Army's 83rd Infantry Division) was heading up the Brittany peninsula," Frank recalled. "At one point, in the village of Pontaubault, we crossed a bridge that spanned a river called the Selune. Down below, on the banks of the river, was a restaurant, and in front of the restaurant there was a beautiful Atlantic salmon, hanging from a hook. I can see it in my mind clear as day; it's stuck with me all these years. I remember thinking as we raced on, 'I wish I could stop and find a fly rod and try to catch one of those magnificent fish.' It took me away from where I was to a very different realm. It didn't last long, but for a few moments I was in a different place."

This past May, Frank had the chance to return to Pontaubault with Jeanne and his son Frankie and make a few casts. He was accompanied by a film crew led by John Waller, founder of Uncage the Soul Video Production. "I met Frank while I was producing a short piece on the

North Umpqua for Travel Oregon," Waller said. "I was immediately taken with him. As we got to talking, I asked if there was something he hadn't done yet that he would like to do. His reply was, 'Fly fish the rivers in Normandy that I saw during the war.' I decided I wanted to help make that happen." After initial efforts at securing a single sponsor to underwrite production fell short, Waller turned to crowdsourcing and raised all the money he needed to make the film *Frank Moore: Mending the Line*. (American Airlines, Patagonia, Pro Photo Supply, and the North Umpqua Foundation also contributed to the effort.)

No salmon were found on the trip. Yet it hardly mattered. "As we visited villages along the route that Frank's division marched, hundreds of people thanked him for his service," Waller continued. "Frank was amazing in his ability to express his love and gratitude. It's directed toward everyone he meets. He has the remarkable capacity to make you feel like you're the most special person in the world."

If you ever see a white-haired man approaching an old VW Rabbit on a pullout along the fly-only section of the North Umpqua, pull over and say hello. Odds are good he'll make you feel special too.

When the Roosterfish Start to Run, Anglers Just Try to Keep Up

CABO PULMO, MEXICO—THE SUN WAS HIGH AND HOT AS A GROUP of five fly anglers stood 20 yards above the surf break on a beach near Punta Colorado, peering out into the Sea of Cortez. "What's that?" one of the anglers called out uncertainly, not wishing to raise a false alarm for misidentifying a rock as our quarry. A dark torpedo coalesced in a wave that crested 50 yards offshore, joined soon after by an accomplice on each side.

Soon the fish were accelerating in formation toward the beach. Twenty yards from the sand, one broke left, the others right. The amassed anglers also broke ranks, racing south and north along the beach while desperately trying not to trip over the fly line they were peeling off their reels in an effort to make a successful cast to *el pappagallo*—the roosterfish.

Roosterfish are a member of the jack family and are indigenous to the inshore waters of the eastern Pacific, from Baja California to Costa Rica and Peru. They can reach more than four feet in length and 100 pounds, though 20-pound fish are most common. Roosterfish are marked by one of the sport-fishing world's most unique dorsal fins—a series of seven long spines, its namesake rooster comb.

"Though they're very fast and strong fighters, the greatest appeal roosterfish have is their appearance," said Jad Donaldson, a fly-fishing guide from Oregon who leads trips to Baja. "Roosters are exotic, even sexy—and I don't often use that word to describe fish. They're the Liz Hurley of sportfish, as far as I'm concerned."

While roosterfish have long been pursued with conventional gear in deeper water off the Pacific coasts of mainland Mexico, Costa Rica, and Panama, it is on the East Cape of Baja California where they are within reach from the beach. This region has become the epicenter for fly fishers seeking roosterfish.

The fly-fishing world is perhaps not as attuned as some communities (say, Justin Bieber's fan base) to the wonders of YouTube. Yet the rising popularity of chasing roosterfish can be greatly attributed to a short film by Felt Soul Media called *Running Down the Man*. The film chronicles the exploits of two brothers, Frank and Bill Smethurst, as they set out to smash the hypothesis posited by many peers that roosterfish cannot be caught on a fly rod. Much of the action involves the brothers sprinting up and down the beach in pursuit of their prey—and occasionally hooking and landing them. Snippets of the film posted on YouTube have gone wildly viral—at least by angling standards—and have fostered a new fishery with a decidedly aerobic twist.

A day of roosterfishing on the East Cape means a day on the beach—walking, riding an ATV, or sitting, depending on your preference.

"Fishing for roosters is all sight-fishing, and you need the sun high in the sky," said Bill White, the proprietor of El Pulmo Eco Palapa, an eco-lodge catering to the East Cape's fly-fishing tourists. "Some people will roam the beaches searching for fish on the move, but others opt to find a spot with good visibility and wait for the fish to arrive. The biggest fish we caught in 2009 was by an angler who sat in one spot all day—by a cooler of beer!"

Sometimes, the fish are spotted coming out of the deeper water toward the beach; other times, the roosterfish appear in the trough where waves break on the beach, just a few feet from shore. Once the fish come in to hunt or corral baitfish, the workout begins. Roosters have excellent eyesight, and the fly—a seven-inch baitfish pattern called a rasta—should be presented a bit in front of the fish, and then stripped quickly. When the fish turns right or left, the angler needs to sprint ahead of it to make the cast. This is no small feat when the surf is crashing, the fly line wants to tangle around the rod butt, and the object of the angler's desire is barreling along on a parallel course, sometimes just 30 feet away. (Considering that the wind is often up and in their face, anglers will claim a small victory in managing not to sink the size 2/0 hook into their scalp.)

Sometimes, anglers will get only one shot before the fish retreats to the deep; sometimes, they will get three or four, and find themselves gasping for air 150 yards up the beach from where they started their run-and-gun assault. On this level, the quest for roosterfish is the fly-fishing equivalent of the Olympic biathlon, in which competitors cross-country ski from target to target, pausing briefly to take aim at the bull's-eye.

Having not sprinted since my high school hockey days some 30 years distant, I found myself bent over breathless (but not quite in need of resuscitation) after a few rooster dashes.

My efforts were not completely unrewarded. Several times, smallish roosters (in the 10-pound class) followed the fly nearly to my feet before turning away.

On another occasion, a jack crevalle darted ahead of a group of roosters intent on my rasta and found itself fast to my 10-weight.

Though roosterless this trip, there is an upside: I left inspired to get in better shape before next summer and my next opportunity at running down the man.

Once Considered "Trash," Carp Become Worthy Fly Rod Target

FLY FISH FOR CARP? FOR MANY ANGLERS, THE FIRST RESPONSE TO THIS question might be "Why?" For cold-water anglers, carp have long been the fodder of mean-spirited jokes, a species more likely to be pursued with a bow and arrow than a beadhead nymph. But the fly-fishing frame of mind regarding *Cyprinus carpio* is changing.

Will Rice, an outdoor writer based in Denver, had his moment of "carptharsis" a number of years ago. "During the spring runoff, trout fishing in the Colorado Rockies is just not happening," he said. "One May, a friend and I were eager to wet a line, so we headed east from Denver to fish a reservoir for wiper (a hybrid between striped bass and white bass). We rented a boat and began zipping around. At the edges, high water had pushed over the banks into some grass flats. We took a closer look, and saw all these fish moving around—10- to 12-pound fish—finning, mudding, even tailing. They were carp. We didn't catch any that day, but it was eye-opening to see fish behaving like this—the way bonefish and permit behave. Carp are a species you can sight-cast to with a fly rod without traveling to the Caribbean."

Comparisons to bonefish in terms of their similar skittishness and strength have earned carp the moniker "golden ghost."

Common carp are of the cyprinid family, the largest group of freshwater fish. Distinguished by large, sometimes golden scales, barbels, a stout profile, and a small mouth, carp can grow to over four feet and nearly 100 pounds, though two- to three-foot specimens between 10 and 20 pounds are more commonly encountered in U.S. waters. Lacking the streamlined shape and the delicate watercolor patterns of trout, carp aesthetics are an acquired taste for some. "I think carp are maligned here because they're not considered classic table fare—though they were brought to North America in the 1800s specifically for that purpose," said Kirk Deeter, an editor-at-large for *Field & Stream* and part of a clan of fly fishers who regularly stalk carp in the South Platte River in downtown Denver. "They are one of the most resilient fish in the world. They can live in almost any conditions—warm or cold, clean or dirty water—and are readily accessible just about wherever you live. Go to a local lake or a golf course pond, carp are the fish you're likely to see. If you want to sight-cast to a tailing fish that might be 10 pounds or more, carp are it.

"I like to equate carp fishing with soccer," Deeter added. "Around the world, carp is the number one sport fish. A staggering amount of money is spent on carp angling. But here in America, it's just starting to catch on."

This may be true among casual anglers, but many pros know better. Ask many guides on the finest trout streams in the American West what they do on their days off, and they will sheepishly admit that they chase carp. "There's a pretty common theme for anglers who get excited about carp," Rice continued. "They start out fly fishing for trout, and then take a saltwater trip where they catch bonefish and tarpon. In the course of the saltwater fishing, something clicks about getting bigger fish on the fly. When they get back home and fish for trout again, that big-fish thrill is a little lacking. Then they discover carp."

Carp are catholic feeders; they'll feast on aquatic insects in all life stages, crayfish, baitfish, and even plant matter, such as blackberries. Anglers shouldn't mistake the carp's broad appetite as license for sloppy presentations. Carp possess highly developed senses of sight, hearing, touch, and smell. This makes them extremely spooky. A spooked fish emits a pheromone that warns other nearby fish of potential danger. If you misfire and put one fish off, odds are good that any other fish in the immediate region will go off the bite as well. "On the South Platte, I believe the fish are mostly eating crawfish, so I rely on crawfish or crab imitations," Rice continued. "I use the same crab patterns that I use for permit. In the end, it's all about watching the take. Seeing a nice carp suck up a fly is always a thrill. When you set the hook, they don't even know what's going on; they just continue on their way. When they do realize that something's wrong, the water explodes, and they're gone. The big ones roll off slowly like an 18-wheeler in low gear. The smaller fish can melt line off the reel."

"Before I had a family, fishing meant going to the end of the road and bushwhacking as far back into the woods as I could," said Chris Wood, President and Chief Executive Officer of the conservation organization Trout Unlimited. "The further back you go, the fewer people and the better the fishing. Now, one of my favorite places to go is the C&O Canal in Washington, D.C. I take my sons out with me and we fish from the towpath, and we catch some big carp. When the Texas mulberry trees are ripe with berries and the berries are dropping in the water, the fish will take them on the surface. We use mulberry patterns and fish them like dry flies. If the hatch is on, it's as exciting as catching bonefish."

Seeking Stripers in the Shallows of Maine's Casco Bay

PORTLAND, MAINE—I WAS STANDING IN THE BOW OF A LOW-RIDING skiff as my angling companion poled us across white sand flats, illuminated by a warm summer sun. Suddenly several V-wakes appeared before the boat. My companion called out from the poling platform at the stern, "Forty feet, one o'clock—drop it on 'em!" As I backcast, a lobster boat chugged across our path, and distinctive Downeast accents could be heard over the diesel engine. Releasing the fly line, I was reminded that I wasn't seeking bonefish in the Bahamas, but casting to skinny-water striped bass on Maine's Casco Bay.

"I've been a striped bass angler since I was a boy," said Mac McKeever, a senior public relations representative at L.L.Bean and my Maine angling companion. "But I've also long been fascinated with shallow-water flats fishing, like you find in the Caribbean. The visual element, the challenge of making a very precise fly presentation, are both very compelling. I didn't think such fishing was available around Maine, and in the past would spend thousands of dollars and lots of time to travel to the Florida Keys or the Bahamas. My pursuit of stripers was typical of most other anglers—blind-casting off beaches, ledges, and tidal rips in hopes of ambushing passing fish.

"One day I was putting my boat on the trailer after a morning of fishing and got to chatting with a utility lineman who was having lunch by the boat launch. He mentioned a spot not far away where he'd watched big schools of large stripers patrolling an area of shallow water from his vantage point at the top of a telephone pole high on a bluff.

I thanked him, backed my boat back into the water and raced over to the spot. Sure enough, the fish were there. The clear water, combined with the white sand and dark fish, made for great visuals. It was very exciting to discover a fishery that was comparable to the exotic locales to the south so close to home."

Casco Bay stretches east and north some 220 square miles from Portland. While not quite Downeast Maine in terms of location, it has the rocky coastline and pine-dotted coves that define the state for many visitors. Despite being in the shadow of the Pine Tree State's largest city, Casco Bay has maintained much of its wild flavor; you're as likely to be accompanied by seals and porpoises as you move from flat to flat as you are other anglers. Though it's near the northern boundary of the striper's range, several factors bring fish to the region from May through October. The bay is fed by a number of rivers, which attract a host of forage fish, including herring, alewives, smelt, and eel. Beyond the river mouths, Casco Bay offers nearly 15,000 acres of mud and sand flats, with powerful 7- to 13-foot tides cycling fresh water (and fresh bait) through the region throughout the day. "There are countless channels that run through the flats, and you can follow the tide changes for a long time," said Captain Eric Wallace, who operates Coastal Fly Anglers, a guide service out of Freeport. "The stripers are social creatures, and one small group will take up with another until you have quite a group of fish assembled."

Back in the late 1970s, striped bass populations in Maine—and throughout their range on the Eastern Seaboard—plummeted to levels that threatened the species' viability. Populations rebounded after the coastwide moratorium on recreational and commercial fishing established by the Atlantic States Marine Fisheries Commission in the 1980s, but the last decade has seen fish numbers once again decline significantly. "The decline has to a great extent been caused by problems in the Chesapeake Bay, where the majority of Maine's migratory stripers are spawned," said Duncan Barnes, Chairman of the Maine Chapter of the Coastal Conservation Association. "Those problems include mycobacteriosis (a wasting disease that has affected the majority of stripers in the Chesapeake Bay and will be fatal to most of those fish), overfishing of menhaden (a prime striped bass forage species), and poor water quality. Thanks to pressure from the Coastal Conservation Association and other striped bass advocacy groups, the Atlantic States Marine Fisheries Commission recently voted to consider reducing striped bass mortality caused by sport and commercial fishermen coastwide and better regulate commercial menhaden fishing."

On the morning I fished, there was certainly no shortage of stripers—though enticing them to take my crab pattern was another matter. Nice-sized fish—10 to 20 pounds—turned to look at the fly. Several even picked it up for closer examination, all in plain view from my position on the bow of Mac's flats skiff. Yet the line never came tight. "Stripers on the flats are a completely different animal than the fish you encounter crashing into bait balls," McKeever continued. "They're hyperwary and extremely skittish. I've had hard-core bonefish anglers on these flats, and they're amazed at how finicky the stripers can be."

"This kind of fishing is more challenging than other striped bass methods," said guide Eric Wallace, who also works on the flats of the Keys. "You've got to cast very accurately, using a long leader and fairly light tippet. Anglers have to react quickly, as the window to make the presentation is brief."

But the challenge makes it all worthwhile. "For every 20 stripers I hook blind-casting, I would rather catch one sight-fishing," McKeever added. "It's a more fulfilling way to fish."

Nato and the Human Anchor

The first time I fished with Nato, he was wearing a pair of cream-colored Dolce & Gabbana track pants and a tan Simms shirt. His natty ensemble was set off by a dark blue fanny pack, which brought to mind a cummerbund. Combined with his slim physique (I'd guess Nato tips the scales at less than 120 pounds) and pencil-thin John Waters moustache and preternaturally white teeth (given that Nato is somewhere north of 60), the overall affect was that of a toreador.

And the permit of Chetumal Bay were his bull.

There are guides that make an effort to gage the ability of their clients, to grasp the sort of experience they're seeking. Some may even attempt to lend the day a certain narrative arc.

Nato was not that sort of guide. He possessed a single-mindedness of purpose. Nato wanted to catch permit. And it's my sense that he viewed any anglers in the boat as an impediment, rather than a means, to that end. This attitude was manifested in several ways during my visit to Xcalak, at the southern tip of the Yucatán Peninsula:

- A general refusal to point out the location of any fish that he'd spotted beyond the point of a finger and a gruff "don't you see it/them?" No o'clock, no distance, no nothing.
- An obvious disgust with the angler if he or she happened to muff a cast, expressed by either a muffled curse or a clutch of his temples in a Munch-like gesture of despair/bafflement/angst.

After one such lost opportunity when I left an 80-plus-foot shot a few feet short, Nato said, "Get down." I pointed to the water, thinking he wanted to pursue our quarry on foot, as we'd done earlier in the day. The dismissive shake of his head made it clear that he simply wanted me off the casting platform, though my fishing partner had been on deck for the last hour and I'd come up only 10 minutes before. I'd been that disappointing.

Understanding my shortcomings, I was willing to entertain the possibility that Nato simply had it out for me. A casual sampling of the other members of my party dispelled this notion. One very competent female angler came off Nato's boat nearly in tears; he had neglected to speak to her during the entire course of the day, directing any comments to the angler's husband. Another guest—one of the most gentle, easygoing men I've ever met—commented on his day with Nato by saying, "I wanted to throw him off the boat after the first five minutes."

Nato was not everyone's idea of a people person. But to give him his due, Nato's anglers did catch permit. Of seven fish landed during eight days of angling by seven guides and a dozen anglers, three came to his boat. When the third fish was tailed, Nato exclaimed, "Another permit for Nato!" according to the angler holding the rod who mistakenly believed that he'd hooked, fought, and landed the fish.

Nato was not alone in his at times quixotic pursuit of Xcalak's permit. He was accompanied each day by a man named Chucho. Chucho might be characterized as the Sancho Panza to Nato's Don—he's a bit chunkier, he showed up for work more modestly attired in shorts and an off-brand fishing shirt, and he sported a regulation moustache. While I wouldn't say that Chucho is Nato's servant, he's certainly not an equal . . . at least not out on the water. He assumed several roles during our outings. First, he helped Nato pole the panga. (Both men pole, eschewing fiberglass or graphite poles in favor of weathered limbs of white mangrove, with Nato in the front and Chucho in back; Chucho provided most of the muscle, Nato the nuance.) Second, he would fire up the motor and pilot the boat on short runs to new fishing grounds when Nato thought it more prudent to maintain his vantage point at the bow.

And, he would serve as Nato's human anchor.

This was not the first time I'd witnessed the human anchor concept. On some Montana rivers, guides will step out of the drift boat and walk it through a promising stretch of water to give their sports more casts and a better drift. On Ascension Bay, at least one lodge (Palometa Club) employs two guides per boat in their pursuit of permit. Once fish are spotted, one guide may accompany the angler on foot while the other anchors the boat and tracks the permits' progress across the flat from the poling platform, calling out directions as needed. On occasions, a guide might jump over the side and hold the boat while the other directs the angler, if the current or wind makes it too challenging to anchor with the pole.

Chucho's anchoring role—as choreographed by Nato—seemed more arbitrary, and certainly more one-sided, than previous human anchor scenarios I'd witnessed. Montana guides *choose* to step out of the boat; Palometa's guides share the role of spotter/holder. Nato *never* dropped into the brine to hold the boat. And adding insult to injury, he'd direct Chucho's anchoring endeavors with sharp and increasingly urgent hand gestures, not unlike a catcher expressing frustration with a promising yet unproven closer . . . or a dog handler dealing with an especially slow schnauzer. Even the directive to get in the water was expressed with an impatient downward motion of the index finger. Chucho was not a tall man, and more often than not, he was up to his chin in the salt, his head bobbing above the water like that of a plaintive otter as he pushed the panga forward, left or right, per Nato's motions . . . and in my case, all for naught.

Staring into the infinite glare of rippling Chetumal Bay as Chucho edged us along, seldom if ever seeing the permit that Nato claimed to see, I found myself experiencing a vertigo of sorts. In my slightly dizzy state, I imagined a runway in Paris or Milan, with a string of slight, pencil-thin mustachioed men voguing and primping in the latest designer guide pants, white teeth flashing in the klieg lights.

The floor below was populated by a sea of Chuchos, only their heads visible in the darkness, illuminated by the fluorescence of the runway.

Postcard from Homosassa

Just as trout aficionados long to one day voyage to the Railroad Ranch section of the Henry's Fork for Opening Day, anyone who has seriously pursued tarpon dreams of fishing the flats of greater Homosassa in May and June for a chance to hook into a "giant" tarpon (a fish of 120 pounds or more), or a "toad that pushes the mark" (a tarpon approaching the mythic weight of 200 pounds, in the local parlance). For six weeks or so, the locals—salt-of-the-earth folks who might feel at home in a Kid Rock video—are joined by middle-aged men in bright-colored, UV-resistant fishing shirts, toting large arbor reels that cost more than some of the cars in the Publix parking lot where everyone gathers to buy ice.

If you're looking for a chance to land a world-record tarpon on a fly, Homosassa has been the place to go.

It was on the flats of Homosassa that the first giant tarpon was landed on a fly. The angler was Lefty Kreh; the year, 1971. A long procession of saltwater-angling luminaries, inspired by tales of Lefty's success, soon followed, among them Norman Duncan, Steve Huff, Stu Apte, and Billy Pate. By the late '70s, word was officially out. "Back in the good old days, it was not unheard of for the best anglers to jump 50 fish in a day," my buddy Mac McKeever shared during one of the long phone conversations leading up to my first visit. "You don't hear reports like this anymore, but the big fish are still around. An angler named Jim Holland Jr. landed a 202.5-pound fish in 2001, just north of town. I've seen fish pushing 200 pounds swim right past my boat. To know that your fly is a few feet away from a fish like that is incredibly exhilarating . . . whether they eat it or not. When they do eat, it's remarkable."

"I see fish almost every year that might eclipse the world record," said Captain Jim Long, an alligator trapper turned guide who's been leading anglers to tarpon for almost 25 years. "Billy Pate put it well—'Your next cast could be to a world record.' At how many places can you say that?

"He also said, 'I never hooked a bad tarpon. Some are just bigger than others.'"

Everyone agrees that the giant tarpon that frequent the Homosassa region each spring are migratory fish . . . though no one knows exactly why they come. One popular conjecture is that the infusion of fresh water from the cool, clear rivers that feed into the Gulf of Mexico here has a lot to do with it. The theory goes that the mix of fresh and salt water creates an ideal habitat for crabs, which the fish seem to target. Another popular belief is that the fish no longer come to Homosassa in significant numbers—whether it's because the amount of fresh water running into the salt has changed, making the area less hospitable to crabs, or simply because there's too much fishing pressure.

I visited greater Homosassa this past spring, expecting to encounter a rich angling history and a paltry present. I was very wrong on one count.

After a 20-minute run from the Homosassa River, guide Jim Farrier killed the outboard and switched on his trolling motor as we began to cut across Chassahowitzka Bay. "Back in the day, Dan Malzone (who still guides out of the Tampa area) and others fished out of Bayport, near Pine Island," he shared while scanning the bay for "blooping" fish. "They'd pole from the front of the boat, but they didn't have to pole far. There would be 200 fish around the Oklahoma Flats. You'd go five feet, cast, hook and land a fish, or hook and break it off. You wouldn't have to move far to find another. Back then, you'd choose a fish and cast. Now you throw it at the group and hope."

This was the sort of "should've been here 20 years ago" lore I had expected, and scanning the four-foot-deep flats, I tried to imagine a time when tarpon swarmed here. When a huge pod presented itself, dorsal fins audibly slicing through the water as the fish porpoised, I thought it was a reverie. The school—at least 30 fish, perhaps 50—daisy-chained 50 yards in front of the boat, and my fellow angler, longtime Sage rep

Raz Reid, stepped up to cast. "Tarpon angling is an important market for Sage," he offered, in between shots. "It's not a big market, but it's a showcase for performance."

For the next two hours, we followed the school up and down a sandbar in the middle of the bay. The fish would chain up, one of us would cast, the fish would ignore our offerings, disperse, and appear again 200 yards ahead or to the left or right. We tried seven, eight, nine different patterns, with no takers. "I've seen times out there when big schools will lollygag around at the top, but won't eat for anything. It's because there are sharks around," Farrier explained. Before we could attach fly number 10, one, two, then four large bull sharks materialized along the periphery of the school, dwarfing the 100-pound tarpon. Not long after, the school departed. Farrier motored toward a spot called "The Point" at the northwest corner of Chassahowitzka Bay. We anchored up and waited to ambush fish heading past on the outgoing tide with the other members of our group, including guides John Bazo and Kyle Messier and anglers Jeff Fryhover (of Umpqua Feather Merchants) and Mac McKeever and Mike Gawtry (both from L.L.Bean). Not many fish came by, but the whole group was encouraged by the schools we'd all pursued through the morning, albeit unsuccessfully.

I spent the next day in the boat with Will Brundick, who had a recently minted captain's license, and is the junior member of Homosassa's guide corps. Though new to the game, Will showed both great enthusiasm and a good deal of promise. Fishing tarpon fills an important slot in a working guide's calendar; a seasoned guide like Jim Long can book upwards of 50 days during the two-month season. ("It can be like my yearly bonus," Long told me later.) Brundick logs most of his guide hours leading sports to redfish back in the marshes at this stage of the game, though he aspires to make tarpon a bigger part of his spring. "There's an unofficial code of ethics out here among the guides," he explained as he poled us parallel to the pole line that extends from the shoreline some seven miles out into the Gulf. "If I'm on a school and one of the guides that are out hunting records, like Steve Kilpatrick and Tom Evans, comes up—or even one of the more seasoned guides like Jim Long or John Bazo—I'll leave the fish." This sort of respect has fostered an apprentice program of sorts. "I always try to help new guides learn the ropes," Long offered. "Some people have told me that I shouldn't be so willing to help, but I figure that maybe the guy I help won't screw up my fishing another day. Ignorance is one thing; arrogance is another. Some of the Keys guides that used to come up here were a little less respectful of their fellow guides, though the great ones were. There's always going to be one bad apple in the bunch." Long helped found the Homosassa Guide's Association a few years back to help buff up potential bad apples. "The HGA has created a standard of good ethics and professionalism, on the water and off, that everyone should live up to," said Daryl Seaton, who operates the Best Western Crystal River Resort and the Nature Coast Fly Shop. "If the first thing a visitor sees is a guide behaving badly, it tarnishes everybody."

In the early '90s, there were over 50 guides working the waters of Greater Homosassa during the tarpon season. Thanks to the fishery's decline—or, in the last few years, the perceived decline—the fleet is now down to a dozen or so boats.

My day with Captain Brundick mirrored the previous day with Jim Farrier. Poling around Chassahowitzka Bay, we saw a number of fish, but found no eaters. At The Point, our group watched an angler fishing solo jump what looked to be a 100-plus-pound fish. He lifted anchor and fought the fish for half an hour. He slowly faded into the distance, and we never saw a fish raised to the boat.

NOTE: Given the vicissitudes of tarpon fishing and the fact that few fish are actually landed, guides and anglers have devised a special lexicon to measure modest levels of success. These include "jump" (when a fish is hooked, however briefly, and leaves the water); "eat" (when guide and/or angler see the fish open its mouth in an attempt to eat the fly, but fish and angler never connect); and "lean" (when a guide and/or angler see the fish move toward the fly, but not actually open its mouth in an attempt to eat the fly).

With ever-increasing gains in sonar and brain-scanning technology, one can imagine that soon captains will be able to monitor and measure "thinks," deducing that a fish has thought about your fly but decided not to act upon that thought.

Before daybreak the following morning, I stepped into Jim Long's Silver King skiff and we pushed off from McRae's Marina. The Dawn Patrol. The Silver King is the boat of preference among Homosassa's guide corps. It has a little broader beam that most modern flats boats, and a lot more weight—200 extra pounds. This makes them a bear to pole, but a lot more stable in the kind of open-water tarpon-fishing situations one encounters around Homosassa.

The three current world-record tarpon caught in Homosassa came out of Silver Kings.

"I don't know if people can smell tarpon," Long ventured as we zipped past The Point into Chassahowitzka. "I had a client who claimed he could." Jim Long has a long Homosassa pedigree. He's one of the bridges between the days of lore and the present, a present that's not quite ready to be dismissed. "Nat Raglan took me under his wing in the '80s," he continued. "He taught me to tie flies and leaders. Nat was a Keys guide, and I met him at the Bayport Inn where the out-of-town tarpon guides would stay. I caught my tarpon on a fly rod with Mike Locklear on a fly I tied that was a variation of the Black Death. When I showed Mike the fly, he said, 'It's not perfect.' After I caught a fish on it, he asked me to tie two or three up for him."

That morning, the odds were beginning to look in our favor. As the sun brightened the expanses of the bay, three distinct pods of tarpon could be seen blooping, porpoising, and otherwise exposing their whereabouts. Long, my angling partner Jeff Fryhover, and I closed in on one group. Fryhover assumed what Long called "the Billy Pate ready position": hook of the fly in line hand, index finger on line in the rod hand. He had several good shots, but no takers. "When I started guiding, my work clothes were boots and jeans, my uniform for trapping gators," Long said as we patrolled the bay with an electric trolling motor, searching for the next pod of fish. "I looked like I was fixin' to climb on a tractor." Occasional reports from other guides filtered in over the radio and Long's cell phone—a lot of fish were being sighted, with few being hooked . . . though one boat had landed two fish at the back of the bay.

"2011 was the best year we had since the '80s in terms of the numbers of fish around," Long offered. "2012 has the markings to be just as good.

It's not like the old days, but then nothing is. Even in the bad years, I felt like the fishing was manageable. There were tarpon around, but it was hard for people who didn't spend lots of time here [e.g., the guides coming in from out of town] to find them."

When I later asked Dr. Kathy Guindon, Assistant Research Scientist with the Florida Fish and Wildlife Conservation Commission and the Commission's lead tarpon biologist, about the tarpon returns for 2012—and prospects for 2013—she paused. "We don't really have a way to assess tarpon stocks, as very few fish are harvested, and stock assessments are generally done with data gleaned from dead fish," she explained. "In the '50s and '60s, there were more catch-and-kill tourneys and higher tarpon harvest rates than there are today, but fortunately the ethos has changed." In 1989, Florida required anglers to purchase a $50 harvest tag for any tarpon they wished to kill. "That first year, 961 harvest tags were sold," Guindon continued. "The past few years, it's been averaging less than 350. Most of the sold tags are not used."

While hard data on recent fish returns is unavailable, Guindon can say that tarpon stocks are not what they were 50 or 60 years ago. "Commercial fishing records from that time show that there were a lot of fish being harvested in Central and South America," she said. "Considering it takes 10 years for tarpon to reach spawning age, the impact was considerable. But now, new regs are coming into play on a more global basis. Belize is now catch-and-release for tarpon, and Mexico is trying to get changes in place. Right now, we're in a nice phase for tarpon. In the Tampa–St. Petersburg region where I'm based, we're seeing a good mixture of size/age class in the schools we're observing. That's a good sign. I'm optimistic about the future. Though I will say that since I started my research in 2003, the fishing pressure has increased. Technology advances have made it easier to share information quickly, and that brings more people."

I asked Captain Long about the record-seekers, the small cadre of anglers who come each year for one, two, even four weeks, in hopes of finding their way into the record books. Some of these hyperfocused anglers will book their favorite guide for a whole month and rent a house where the two of them will hole up, essentially establishing a two-man tarpon SWAT team. They will spend hours each week testing the breaking strength of their leaders. They will seek out fish that seem to have potential to be world records, and will generally only cast to such fish—though they may cast to smaller tarpon now and again to test fly patterns, quickly breaking the fish off if they take. "I have a couple record-hunters that fish with me," Long continued. "I tie all my materials to IGFA standards, and carry a tarpon kill tag if we think we have a record. I will not force an angler to kill a tarpon if I believe it's a record. But I won't disallow it. It's the angler's day."

A little before lunchtime, our group finally got on the board. As we passed John Bazo's boat, not 100 yards away, we watched McKeever cast, strip, and come tight. The fish, a respectable 75 or 80 pounds, was in the air five or six times before coming to the boat, each leap long and high enough for even an amateur photographer like myself to get a few good photos. The following morning, Gawtry and Long would find a fish twice that size, landing it in just 20 minutes.

After McKeever's fish was landed, the fish ceased rolling. As we'd started the day quite early, I assumed that our day was about done. Long was poling us along and I was on the deck when he said quietly, "Look to the left. There are some fish laid up." Thirty-five or 40 feet out, I could make out five or six fish, hovering near the bottom in about six feet of water. One of the fish seemed very big, with a girth like a giant channel catfish. "I want you to drop the fly on top of them delicately, like you're casting a dry fly to a trout." "Delicate" is not the first adjective I'd use to describe my cast with the 12-weight and a 2/0 Toad pattern, but I tried . . . and my gentler approach left the fly about five feet short. "Again. Further!" Long cajoled. Hell-bent on not leaving the fly short, I overshot the mark slightly on the next cast, with the line, rather than the fly, touching down on the water above the fish. They slowly finned away, not spooked, it seemed, so much as mildly aggravated. Seeing the flanks of the biggest fish, my jaw dropped.

"I didn't want to say anything," Long spoke quietly, "but I think the big one was pushing 180, 190 pounds." I began to apologize for mucking up an easy shot at a truly outsized fish, but Long cut me short. "Nat Raglan told me once, 'Jimmy, when someone makes a bad cast, you don't have to tell them. They know, and they also know you worked hard to get them there. The best thing you can say is, 'That's okay, let's get the next one.'"

POSTSCRIPT: As this story was going to press, we learned that Captain Will Brundick died in a tragic accident at his home, ten days short of his 33rd birthday.

In Ireland, Fishing for Salmon That Like a Crowd

BALLINA, IRELAND—ROTATING MY TWO-HANDED ROD AND SNAPPING it forward, I unfurled a long cast across the Ridge Pool on the River Moy, the most desirable beat on Ireland's most prolific Atlantic salmon river. As my fly, a #12 Cascade with double hooks, swung across the current, salmon rolled in the river before me, at once beguiling and maddening. I took two steps downstream and prepared to cast again, but my concentration was broken by a series of staccato beeps from a procession of cars passing over Upper Bridge downstream. "It's a wedding party," Bryan Ward, an angling officer with Inland Fisheries Ireland, explained. A not uncommon occurrence in downtown Ballina, where wild salmon blend seamlessly with town life.

The River Moy rises in the Ox Mountains of County Sligo in northwest Ireland and flows 62 miles, initially in a southwesterly direction before turning north and entering the Atlantic at Killala Bay, County Mayo. It's perpetually tea-colored waters—thanks to the presence of peat deposits along much of its course—host impressive numbers of returning Atlantic salmon each spring and summer. In a good year, fisheries managers estimate that 75,000 salmon—all wild—return to the Moy, with 30 percent being multi-winter fish and 70 percent grilse (fish that spend only one year at sea, and hence are smaller). Commercial drift-netting off the west coast of Ireland negatively impacted fish returns on the Moy in the past. "Many of the fish we'd see had net marks," said Markus Müller, Fisheries Information Manager for Inland Fisheries Ireland, "and some had their dorsal fins completely scraped away." Drift netting was banned off Ireland shores in 2007, and dividends are beginning to show in western rivers in the shape of increasing fish returns.

Drift nets have been only the first obstacle facing the Moy's salmon as they attempt to reach their natal waters to spawn. In the '60s, much of the river was dredged as part of a scheme to improve land drainage for agricultural purposes. "The drainage scheme probably wouldn't have been allowed on the basis of cost-benefit analysis, but such was the strength of political pressure from farming groups," said Declan Cooke, Moy Fishery Manager. The dredging ripped much of the integrity of the river's substrata away, creating the equivalent of a featureless canal through much of its course. "I have no doubt that the Moy would be significantly more productive if it hadn't been dredged," Cooke continued. "But owing to the well-being of the many tributary streams that feed into the main channel—some of which have been rehabilitated by Fisheries Boards using weirs, deflectors, and spawning gravel—it is still quite a productive river."

Thanks in part to its appeal to European aristocrats in centuries past, Atlantic salmon fishing has been dubbed the sport of kings. Given the finite number of rivers that hold fishable populations of salmon, the opportunity to cast a line over pooling salmon can often demand kingly sums. On most Atlantic salmon rivers, one cannot merely show up and begin casting. Instead, you must lease a "beat," which entitles you to fish a section of river for a predetermined amount of time. Daily beat fees can approach $500 or more on some of Norway and Iceland's most famed rivers. Given its fecundity, beats on the Moy are quite reasonable, ranging from €20 to €120 per half-day session; many beats come with the services of a ghillie (fishing guide). There are beats that might summon an American's notions of idyllic County Mayo countryside, yet the river's most sought-after waters are in downtown Ballina, and include the Ash Tree Pool, Cathedral beat, and Ridge Pool.

For salmon anglers accustomed to the solitude of the deep woods of New Brunswick, an afternoon on the Ridge Pool might prove unsettling. Behind the top of the pool rests an office of Inland Fisheries Ireland, where local ghillies might grab a cup of coffee as you assess your tackle; further downstream, there's the Ballina Manor Hotel. Across the river is

Ridge Pool Road, with assorted storefronts (including two tackle shops) and a promenade where passersby may pause to critique your casting form. During my visit, the water was high enough so that there was no riverbank per se; I stepped off a neatly cobbled sidewalk into the river. (I played golf at several of the wild and wooly links courses in County Mayo during my visit—Enniscrone and Carne—and noticed that the settings of fishing and golf have been inverted here vis-á-vis American paradigms. It's the river, not the golf course, that's immaculately groomed!)

Entering the river, I took my place in a conga line of anglers—six of us in all—spaced every 50 yards throughout the pool. It's proper etiquette for each angler to cast, take two steps, cast, take two steps, etc.—and then return to the top of the pool and proceed through again. Grilse swirled around my line, occasionally clearing the water completely as I marched through the Ridge Pool once, and then again. None were interested in my Cascade fly. As I stepped out of the water near the foot of Upper Bridge, the sun dipped behind the Fisheries building. Glancing upstream at my fellow anglers, I decided that a pint of Guinness at V.J. Doherty's Ridge Pool Bar by Upper Bridge (est. 1913 by the current owner's great-grandfather) would be preferable to another rebuff by the Moy's salmon.

On Our Own on Alaska's Kanektok River

Among Alaska's angling cognoscenti, the Kanektok has long enjoyed a stellar reputation for its seclusion, scenery, and angling. (Insiders simply refer to the Kanektok as "The Chosen.") The river flows roughly 100 miles from its source at Pegati Lake, coursing westward between the Kilbusk and Akhlun Mountains and the tundra of the Yukon Delta National Wildlife Refuge, before meeting the Bering Sea. Fish encountered here include Dolly Varden, arctic char, all five species of Pacific salmon, and, perhaps most famously, "leopard" rainbow trout, so nicknamed for their fine round spots.

There's a reason the Kanektok has remained so spectacular: the only way to fish it is to fly into the lake on a bush plane outfitted with pontoons and then float a raft the 100 miles to the mouth. Anglers can opt for a weeklong guided excursion, which will run about $4,000 per person; or, you can hire an outfitter to fly you in and provide the raft and any other gear you might need and go it on your own, for roughly $4,000 total.

My fishing buddies Pete Gyerko and Geoff Roach and I opted for the latter. Though cost was a consideration, we mainly wanted to go it alone for the sense of adventure such a trip inspired. Catching fish until our arms hurt was one thing; surviving possible grizzly bear encounters, the elements, and any other hardships the river might throw at us was another.

Did I mention that one of the hardships would be the absence of any beer?

Steve Powers of Papa Bear Adventures, who we'd retained as an outfitter, was adamant about the 1,200-pound weight limit for the de Havilland Beaver that would fly us in. Considering that the three of us were pushing 650 pounds—and that the raft and cooler totaled another 250 pounds—we didn't have much room to spare. The cases of microbrews I'd imagined didn't even make the first cut on our extensive packing list. Steaks and ice were out too. After many menu revisions, multiple weigh-ins at home, and sometimes heated debate ("Do we really need two pounds of couscous?"), we arrived in Bethel, thinking we were under weight. But the scale said we were still 78 pounds over. Backup food, box wine, and spare waders were tossed aside; still ten pounds over. Lose the toilet seat or the bug tent. With the mosquitoes already gnawing on our ankles, the toilet went. One pound over. "Go light on breakfast," Powers said, and we started in on the box wine and repacked our dry bags.

The next morning we boarded the Beaver, and pilot Boris Forester flew east. As we sailed above the clouds, Forester said, "I think we must be above the lake, but I want to be sure." We circled just above mountain peaks for a few minutes. When a small opening in the clouds appeared, Boris shot down. Soon we were skimming the lake's surface. Below our pontoons, red shapes darted—sockeye salmon that had reached the lake to spawn. Boris coasted to the shoreline, and we unloaded our gear. He edged the Beaver out of the shallows, waved goodbye, and accelerated off into the clouds.

We were truly on our own.

As we began our float, we were struck by the abundance of fish life. For a solid 15 miles we drifted over school after school of pink salmon—hundreds of thousands, if not millions of fish. This abundance of salmon badly hampered our angling efforts—it was impossible to get a fly to the arctic char and Dolly Varden we hoped to hook, as each cast snagged a salmon. By the next morning the pinks had thinned out, and Geoff had tied on an egg pattern. (The Kanektok's non-salmon species favor salmon eggs when the salmon are spawning . . . and salmon flesh when the spawning is done.) Within a cast or two, Geoff's rod was throbbing violently, and he called out. I've seen Geoff catch many large fish in silence, and ran to see what was on the end of his line. He pointed across the river to the trip's first grizzly. The bear—a modestly sized 500 or 600 pounds—was combing the shore for salmon carcasses and seemed indifferent to our presence. A few times he raised his head to sniff the air, but soon returned to scavenging.

Seeing the bear seemed to alter our luck. That day, we caught arctic char and Dolly Varden at will—30, 40, 50 apiece. Some were pushing 25 inches and five or six pounds, brilliantly mottled in black, gold, and orange. We found a beautiful campsite that looked out at a mountainside dotted with stands of blueberries. As Pete served up a fine meal of spaghetti with pesto (washed down with low weight/high octane scotch), a mother grizz and her cubs slowly picked their way from bush to bush methodically eating their fill. With the sun still high in the sky at 10 p.m. and a warm breeze blowing upriver to keep the bugs at bay, it couldn't get much better.

The float settled into a comfortable routine. Wake up, wader up, make breakfast, break camp, fish our tails off, make camp, make dinner, toast the day, and go to sleep. Though there were copious signs of grizzlies at every gravel bar we waded—scat, half-devoured salmon, very large paw prints—we had no more close encounters. As the river widened and braided up in its lower stretches, we found more and more of the Kanektok's famed leopard rainbows, which aggressively grabbed our flesh flies that we cast up against the omnipresent willows. We also found more and more silver (Coho) salmon, with freshly landed fish finding their way to the frying pan.

It was not always easy going. Our tent stakes were next to useless on the gravel bars, and we had to tie our tents down to driftwood and weigh the sides with hundreds of pounds of gravel each night. Despite such precautions, our bug tent imploded during heavy winds on night four. On our last afternoon, Pete realized that he'd been misreading his new GPS all week, and we were actually 10 miles farther away from the take-out place than we'd thought. He rowed like mad to close the gap—and we stumbled upon one of our best fishing spots of the trip. We took turns hooking powerful silvers, fresh from the salt, somersaulting tail over head as they tore backing from our 8-weight outfits as the light leaked from the 11 p.m. sky.

Casting with the Master

FREEPORT, MAINE—THERE ARE NO STRIPED BASS, SMALLMOUTH bass, or brook trout for several miles, yet a short elderly man with a floppy hat is unfurling a bright yellow fly line through the air in tight loops, its flight illuminated by an unseasonably warm March sun. One passerby stops, then another and another as the line sails across a grass field, over a rope demarcating a sidewalk, and finally into the street beyond. "I don't want to hold up traffic," the caster declares, a gap-toothed grin lighting his face. The onlookers laugh.

Lefty Kreh is holding casting court.

If there's a character in the fly-fishing world who holds a rock star cache, it is Bernard "Lefty" Kreh. As a writer, photographer, television personality, and pioneer (he helped popularize saltwater fly fishing), Kreh has been the face of the sport for several generations of anglers. "Lefty has introduced more people to fly fishing than any other angler," said Mac McKeever, a senior public relations manager at L.L.Bean and fishing buddy of Kreh's. "From angling techniques to equipment development to simply being an ambassador for the sport, it's hard to measure his impact."

Even today at age 87, Lefty keeps a hectic schedule, traveling far afield to fish (he's already been to the Yucatán Peninsula in search of permit and will visit Brazil in October to pursue peacock bass), making public appearances, and conducting casting clinics.

His greatest legacy may be the tens of thousands of people he has taught to fly cast.

At its most graceful, casting a fly rod can be an art form—remember Brad Pitt's beautifully flowing casts in *A River Runs Through It*? In the hands of the uninitiated, it can be an exercise in frustration, with line tangling around the rod or puddling impotently at the would-be angler's feet instead of unfurling 30, 50, 75 feet away and dropping delicately on the water. Frustration will often incite anglers to flail the fly rod faster and faster, which only makes matters worse. Many casting instructors promote a technique where the body remains rigid—legs together, right elbow at the side of the body, rod tip high, casting motion moving from ten o'clock to two o'clock and back. Throughout his long career, Kreh has advocated a more fluid approach. "Look at how a good golfer or a baseball player swings," Lefty tells the group that's gathered at his side on the casting range at the L.L.Bean Spring Fishing Weekend. "They don't just use their arms, they use their bodies. Fly casting shouldn't be any different." He goes on to demonstrate: With his right arm at his side, his right foot slightly behind, and the rod cocked at a 45-degree angle, he turns his hips and shoulders. The fly line whips back and forth on a level plane until he stops the rod abruptly on the forward turn. The line again flies over the rope. "I'm 87 years old; I didn't use my elbow or a double haul, and I cast 80 feet. You guys can do this too."

Lefty invites one onlooker to the casting platform for a tutorial. The man makes a few casts. "Your forward cast isn't bad," Lefty intones in his slightly southern Maryland drawl, "but you've got sorry loops on your backcast. People get a dip in their backcast because they use their wrists. That's no way to cast." His casting protégé begins to explain that he generally uses a longer rod, but the cast master cuts him off. "The length of the rod doesn't mean a damn thing," he says. To prove his point, he removes the top half of the rod from the bottom half, strips out 60 feet of line and proceeds to cast it all with just the rod's top section. "Three things you need to know to make good casts," he continues. "If you are right-handed, the right foot should be positioned to the rear. Before beginning a back or forward cast, the casting-hand thumb should be positioned behind the rod handle as it's aimed at the target. Lastly, the elbow should not be elevated on the cast. Think of keeping it on a shelf that's as high as your elbow."

"Lefty's a pure instructor," McKeever added. "There have been many occasions when we've motored up to a boat ramp after fishing and someone recognizes him. By the time I get back with the truck to pull out the boat, he's giving his admirers an impromptu casting lesson. I think he wants people to improve their casts so they can improve their success and get as much enjoyment as possible out of their fishing."

After a few more casters are critiqued, it's my turn. I'd always felt that I had a decent cast, if imperfect technique. Lefty quickly sets me straight. My elbow is straying off the shelf. My rod tip is drifting skyward. My back cast is "sorry." Lefty adjusts the position of the thumb on my casting hand. He lowers the trajectory of my backcast so it's more parallel to the ground. He advises me to stop the progress of my forward cast earlier in the stroke. After a few awkward efforts, a cast flies over the rope onto the sidewalk. "That was a little better," I say, hoping to avoid further admonitions from the cast master.

"That was good," he replies, with that gap-toothed smile.

From Lefty Kreh, that means a lot.

Salmonflies Awaken Western Trout, Anglers

WARM SPRINGS, OREGON—THE SKY WAS NOT EXACTLY DARK IN A biblical blotting-out-the-sun sense, but the Salmonflies were certainly thick above central Oregon's Lower Deschutes River. Thousands of female specimens circled 30 feet above the water's surface, preparing to descend and drop their eggs. Occasionally a bug would spiral slowly down to the river, flutter awkwardly on the surface, and then disappear in a sudden splash.

The Deschutes' native rainbow trout take notice of the Salmonflies' arrival among the river's rimrock walls. And anglers do, too.

For most trout enthusiasts, dry-fly fishing represents the pinnacle of the pastime. Mayflies, caddisflies, and a host of other miniscule insects emerge from the river bottom and make their way to the surface. The trout, which have been feeding on the nymphal forms of the insects lower in the water column, shift their focus to the top, where the bugs float helplessly at the whim of the current. Observant anglers can identify the kind of bug that's emerging and choose a fly pattern that emulates the natural insect—"matching the hatch," in the angler's parlance—and then, if all goes right, enjoy the visceral thrill of watching the trout rise and take the fly in question.

The challenge—at least for anglers of a certain age—is that many aquatic insects, and the flies that imitate them, are considerably smaller than your pinky nail. Identifying one's fly on the water amongst the many natural bugs—or for that matter, tying it on the line—can prove frustrating.

One reason that the Salmonfly hatch brings such joy to the faithful is that these bugs can be the *length* of your pinky, making them visible to even older eyes. Another is that even the wariest trout seem to throw caution to the wind when these insects appear, gorging indiscriminately. "Guided trips for the peak of the Salmonfly season on the Deschutes—from late May through mid-June—are usually booked by the beginning of March," said Damien Nurre, co-owner of Deep Canyon Outfitters, based in Bend, Oregon. "There's a four- or five-day window during the hatch when the fish will eat almost any fly we cast. The Salmonfly hatch is one of those bucket list experiences that people plan for months in advance."

Salmonflies (*Pteronarcys californica*) occur on many western rivers: the Gunnison in Colorado, the Madison in Montana, and Henry's Fork in Idaho, to name a few. Salmonflies spend most of their existence as nymphs, encased in a black shuck and nestled in cracks and crevices in the river bottom. When the river temperatures hit the low 50s in late May or June (exact temperature/timing varies system to system), the nymphs begin their trek to shore, and plant themselves on rocks, tree trunks, and any place else they can gain purchase. Ranging from two to three inches in length with an even longer wingspan and a telltale orange abdomen, Salmonflies represent a significant source of protein; on many river systems, they are the biggest bug the trout will see. During this time, the wind that may sometimes dog the fly anglers' cast can become a friend, blowing the hapless bugs into the water. It's then—and when the females return to the water to deposit their eggs—that the topwater feeding bacchanalia begins.

"In a river like the Deschutes, Salmonflies are a major food source," said Rick Hafele, a writer and aquatic biologist, formerly with Oregon's Department of Environmental Quality. "Because the Salmonfly hatches occur so consistently and there are thousands of bugs emerging at once, the trout key on them. I've hooked fish that had Salmonflies spilling out of their mouths—but they still took my fly. Their stomachs were distended, hard as a rock."

At the height of the Salmonfly hatch, many Deschutes rainbows move up against the river's banks to wait for insects to drop off overhanging branches. This can make for some tricky casting, though the fish are not very particular about delicate presentations. "I like to position anglers downstream from alder trees, where Salmonflies are fluttering about," outfitter Nurre continued. "You want to get the fly as far under the branches as possible, as that's where the fish are waiting for the bugs. It doesn't hurt to slap the fly down, as the natural bugs don't land gently. We use short, stout leaders, so you can yank the fly out of the branches if you hang up. There's a lot of variation in how the trout take the fly. If the current is slower, the fish will come up and inspect the fly. If they're satisfied, they'll suck it down. If the water is moving faster, the takes are more splashy and aggressive, as the fish have less time to make a decision."

The Salmonfly hatch has inspired many notable fly patterns over the years. Early flies, like the Sofa Pillow and the Stimulator, relied on hackle (cock feathers) and elk hair to keep them afloat. "With the traditional patterns, I found that my clients were spending half their time false-casting to dry them off," said Jason Yeager, a commercial fly tier who also guides on the Gunnison in Colorado. "That's time the fly isn't in the water, fishing. I started experimenting with foam. Some didn't think the foam-bodied flies would be effective, but they have a realistic silhouette, and float well, even in the rapids."

One of the more popular patterns on the Deschutes is called the Chubby Chernobyl, a mostly foam fly that bears no clear resemblance to the actual insect. "It shouldn't work," Nurre added. "But it does."

The Fish Whose Bite Is as Fierce as Its Name

SEATTLE—The trucks delivering produce to Pike Place Market were still unloading as Dave McCoy, owner of Emerald Water Anglers, picked me up at my hotel for a day of fishing. Soon we were driving south on Interstate 5. After a quick coffee stop, we headed west across the Tacoma Narrows Bridge and then down a twisting country road. Coming around a bend, the snow-covered Olympic Mountains jutted forth, resembling jagged dollops of meringue. "We get a lot of bigger fish here, and conditions are perfect," McCoy said, easing his rig into a pullout where a logging truck sat idling. We pulled on our waders and scrambled down a steep bank, 6-weight fly rods in hand, eager to feel the hard pull of a Puget Sound sea-run cutthroat trout.

Sea-run cutthroat—also known as coastal cutthroat or bluebacks—range from the streams and estuaries of northern California to the Inside Passage of southeast Alaska. Sea-runs can range in size from 10 to 24 inches, though fish exceeding 20 inches are considered trophy size. Like steelhead, another great sport fish associated with the Pacific Northwest, sea-runs start life in freshwater rivers, and then migrate to the salt where they spend much of their adult lives, returning to fresh water briefly each year to spawn. "At the end of the day, the life cycle of sea-run cutthroat is something of a mystery," McCoy continued, "both in terms of how much time they're in the salt or fresh water, and how far they roam in Puget Sound." But there's no question about the sea-run's appeal as a sport fish. They strike a fly with vigor, deport themselves like a much larger adversary once hooked, and are among the trout family's most beautiful members—sometimes chrome-bright with their namesake red slash marks nearly invisible, other times a blend of yellow and gold and olive green with prominent "cuts" below the gills, like their mountain stream brethren.

Puget Sound encompasses 3,000 miles of coastline, stretching from the city of Olympia in the south to Port Townsend and Whidbey Island in the north, and filling countless bays and inlets on the way. Much of Washington's population—some four million souls—live along or near Puget Sound. It's hardly pristine; the combined ports of Tacoma and Seattle are the second busiest in the country, and there are several Superfund sites within its borders. Still, with the inflow from thousands of creeks and rivers to dilute some of the effluents that reach the sound, and the tidal influence from the Strait of San Juan de Fuca to inject nutrients into the system, Puget Sound supports a healthy population of marine life, including pods of orcas, porpoises, sea lions, and resident Chinook and Coho salmon. "Puget Sound is unique for this part of the world, as it's shielded from the rough conditions of the Pacific by the Olympic Peninsula to the west, yet has the tidal flow to support a great deal of fish life," McCoy added. "I imagine that the vast majority of the people living here are unaware of the sea-run fishery—that you can catch native trout within view of the Space Needle!"

Sea-run cutthroat tend to be found within casting distance of shoreline, in water less than 10 feet deep. Most fishing is done from the beach. Cutts are catholic feeders, foraging on sand lance, sand shrimp, eels, juvenile herring, and chum salmon fry—basically any protein that presents itself. While tempting them to bite is not particularly difficult, finding them can present a challenge, especially given all that shoreline. "On a given day, we may visit anywhere from two to eight beaches," McCoy said. "Where we start will depend on the tides. I prefer to fish out of the wind if possible, as it's easier to cast and spot feeding fish. If you don't find anything after working a stretch of beach, it's time to try a new place. The fish are always moving, and if you stay in the same spot, it's like waiting for lightning to strike."

At our first stop, on a bay near the south end of the Kitsap Peninsula, we waded into the sandy shallows around clam and oyster beds, as seagulls dropped clamshells on the rocks behind us in hopes of securing their breakfast. We started with short casts parallel to the beach, retrieving the fly—a Foul-Free Herring—with long, fast strips to imitate a fleeing baitfish. We gradually gave out more line and directed our casts toward the opposite shore, doing our best to cover the most possible water. Repeating the cycle, we moved west three or four steps at a time, in the shadow of stylish waterfront A-frames. The wind stayed down, and so did the fish. We returned to the truck and moved on.

Making our way north, we scouted several other beaches for signs of fish activity—the splashes of rolling or jumping cutts—but the trout seemed absent. At one point, we fished near the Southworth Ferry Terminal. The Seattle skyline was clearly in view, a reminder that outdoor pursuits needn't be in the wilderness. After a 15-minute ferry ride to West Seattle, we tried our luck at Seahurst Park. By this time, the wind had come up from the west, and the temperature had dropped to near freezing, though the winter sun still shone. With waves threatening to top our waders, McCoy said, "I don't think it's going to happen today."

I concurred. At that point, a hot cup of Seattle's most celebrated beverage held more promise.

White Nights of Salmon

MURMANSK, RUSSIA—MY FLY SKITTERED ACROSS THE CURRENT IN front of our jet boat on the Lower Tomba beat on Russia's Ponoi River, darting erratically as the tension on my line increased. Suddenly there was a violent splash and I felt a significant tug. Then nothing.

"Don't give the fish any line, and don't yank the rod back," advised Max Mamaev, head guide at the Ponoi River Company. "When you feel the weight of the fish, lift gently." I cast again toward the birch-blanketed bank as two peregrine falcons mobbed a white-tailed sea eagle in the sky above. As the fly accelerated below the boat, a fish rose and missed the fly. Then there was a second swirl, and the line came tight. I lifted slowly and was fast to my tenth Atlantic salmon of the day.

On the Ponoi, anglers almost always get a second chance.

The draw of Atlantic salmon for many devotees is, at least in part, the difficulty of catching them. Much of the challenge is borne of the general scarcity of salmon in many river systems that once held sizable runs, and the number of anglers besieging the fish with colorfully named flies in the streams where returns are more stable. (Atlantic salmon spend their first few years in fresh water, go to sea for one or more years where they grow considerably, and return to their natal rivers to spawn. Some will expire after spawning; others will return to the sea for another cycle.) Most anglers will log many hours on the river between fish hooked, an experience that can foster a fatalistic, if not pessimistic, temperament.

The Ponoi, which flows 250 miles through the taiga terrain of Russia's southern Kola Peninsula (below Murmansk), turns the equation of long hours for few fish on its head.

"In the Atlantic salmon world, the Ponoi is one of the crown jewels," said Bill Taylor, President and Chief Executive Officer of Atlantic Salmon Federation, an international conservation organization based in New Brunswick, Canada. "It boasts the most prolific wild runs of Atlantic salmon in the world. Some anglers have a week or two on the river locked in on their calendars, and spend the rest of the year looking forward to the trip. For others, it's a once-in-a-lifetime adventure where fly fishers know they have a shot at landing as many salmon in a week as they could in a lifetime on their home rivers. Thanks to its isolation, the Ponoi faces few of the threats—poor forestry practices, agricultural runoff, open net pen salmon farming, and urbanization—that hamper healthy wild salmon runs in southern Europe, Canada, and the United States."

"Neophyte fly anglers do not gravitate toward Atlantic salmon fishing," said Mollie Fitzgerald, co-owner of Frontiers International Travel in Gibsonia, Pennsylvania. "That's because on most salmon rivers, a week's fishing may be about one great fish hooked. And that can be frustrating. On the Ponoi, even a first-time fly fisherman can get great rewards. There are rivers with bigger fish and a few that have similarly strong catch rates, but for consistent fishing over a long season (late May through early October), nothing compares to the Ponoi. We've been sending anglers there since the camp opened in the early '90s, and catch rates have steadily improved with the cessation of commercial fishing at the mouth, and focused catch-and-release efforts."

During the week of my stay, the 18 anglers at the Ponoi River Company's Ryabaga Camp averaged more than 60 salmon each, fishing roughly eight hours a day for six days. Several anglers caught and released well over 100 fish.

Such frenetic salmon catching comes at a cost. To reach the Ryabaga Camp, anglers must get to Murmansk and then fly two hours in a military-issue Mi-8 helicopter—few people's idea of comfortable conveyance. During prime fishing weeks, lodge fees can eclipse $13,000.

The tea-colored Ponoi is a big river, at some points 300 yards across. Many runs can be fished from shore, though to access some holding water, anglers fish from boats. Guides anchor at the top of a piece of promising water—a "drop," in Ponoi parlance. The upstream angler casts to the right, the downstream angler to the left. After every few casts, the guide releases several yards of anchor rope, "dropping" the boat further into the run. Fourteen-foot, two-handed spey rods are the order of the day on the Ponoi; the long rods allow anglers to make longer casts to cover more water with less effort. Both traditional and tube-style flies are used.

"Whether you're fishing a skating fly or a wet fly, you want to keep it moving, as the salmon like it fast," head guide Mamaev added. "If the current isn't moving the fly quickly enough, try stripping or twitching the fly."

The Ponoi sits above the Arctic Circle at 67 degrees latitude, and from late May through July, the sun never sets. Ardent (or insomniac) anglers can cast through the night on the Ryabaga Camp's home pool, one of the most productive spots on the river. At 11:30 one evening, I stood near the midpoint of the pool. Unseasonably warm weather had brought the thick stands of birch trees lining the river into bud, and fish were steadily leaping clear of the water below me. I unfurled a cast. As the fly swung down, I looked upstream, where another angler was casting. The still present sun's rays glinted off his fly line as it cut through the rapidly cooling air. A jerk on my rod jolted me back to the matter at hand, and a fish cleared the water at the end of my line, shaking the fly free.

I prepared to cast again, confident another fish would be waiting.

Fly Anglers Are Drawn to a Toothy Adversary

Every few years, a new sport fish emerges as the "it" species for fly fishers to target, a creature that was previously unknown to fly anglers. The list has recently included taimen, golden dorado, and mahseer. Though worthy of angler attention, these quarry require lengthy journeys to faraway lands—Mongolia, Bolivia, and India, respectively.

Fly anglers in the upper Midwest—and around the country—have discovered a new species that anglers with conventional gear have long targeted: muskellunge . . . largely thanks to the obsessions and writings of an angler named Robert Tomes.

"Up in northern Wisconsin, everything is about muskies," Tomes said. "It's not only the topic of all angling conversations, but it's the dominant commercial icon—there are muskie bars, muskie tackle shops, muskie motels—it can't be escaped." (In the town of Hayward, one can visit the National Freshwater Fishing Hall of Fame & Museum, which features the Shrine to Anglers, a half-city-block-long and four-and-a-half-story-tall leaping muskellunge.) On a fishing trip many years ago with his dad to Wolf Lake, Tomes caught his first keeper on a Mepps Musky Killer. "That night at the lodge, they brought out a cake in the shape of a muskie to commemorate my good luck," Tomes continued. "An old-timer came over and clapped me on the shoulder and said, 'Son, I've been muskie fishing my whole life; I've never caught a keeper.' I knew then that muskies would be part of my life."

About the time that he caught his first muskie, Tomes was fostering a passion for fly fishing. "I soon made the connection that if you could catch tarpon or trout on a fly, you could probably catch a muskie," he continued. "The first time I ever went muskie fishing with my fly rod, I got a small but legally sized fish. The visual take, the fight, the aura of having caught this elusive and unpredictable predator on a fly—all of this had a powerful appeal."

Alternately described as freshwater barracuda, lake-dwelling tigers, or the fish of ten thousand casts, muskies are the largest members of the pike family. They reside at the top of the food chain in the lakes and rivers they call home, and are built for mayhem—long and lithe for quick bursts of speed, with large jaws outfitted with extra-sharp teeth; in the old days, anglers used to shoot muskies before bringing them in the boat! Fish average 30 to 40 inches (10 to 20 pounds), though 50-inch "trophy" fish (often eclipsing 40 pounds) are encountered each year. Muskies are catholic eaters—in addition to baitfish, they've been known to eat other gamefish, waterfowl, and small mammals.

Given the muskellunge's size and predilection for larger pieces of protein, conventional-gear anglers have often relied on lures that might dwarf the brook trout found in some New England streams. It should be no surprise, then, that the sight of a ribbon of fly line unfolding over a likely muskie lie was met with arched eyebrows if not sniggering laughter by die-hard muskellunge anglers. "My first impression of fly fishing was that small flies equal small fish," said Larry Ramsell, Legendary Angler in the National Freshwater Fishing Hall of Fame & Museum and two-term Past International President of Muskies, Inc. "It also looked like a lot of work. But anglers like Robert have come up with flies and techniques that are more than sufficient for what muskies are looking for, and they can fish shallow, weed-infested areas that guys fishing with large lures just can't get to."

Testimony to the possibilities of fly fishing for the state fish of Wisconsin and its growing acceptance: at the 16th Annual Chicago Muskie Show, the world's largest exhibition for muskellunge devotees, Robert Tomes was a keynote speaker and addressed a roomful of old-guard muskie anglers. "Five years ago, there would have been six guys in the room," Ramsell added.

Fly fishing for muskellunge has its advantages, yet it's not a relaxing exercise. First, it usually means blind-casting a heavy 9- or 10-weight rod from dawn to dusk, throwing large streamers and poppers, some that would seem better suited to bluewater billfishing. You'll have to learn about the places muskies like to lie in wait to ambush prey—weed beds, drop-offs, fallen timber. If you're fortunate enough to entice a fish to take your fly, you'll need to resist the temptation to lift the rod and use a strip set instead.

Most important of all, you need the proper mental preparation.

"You need to maintain a cautious optimism that a fish is going to present itself, even though you've been casting for eight hours and haven't seen a thing," Tomes advised. "You have to imagine that it's going to happen, have a positive visualization of you hooking, fighting, and landing—and, of course, releasing—a muskie. These are moody creatures and seem to know—and strike—the moment you drop your guard. Not everyone can handle that."

Whether one connects with a muskie or not, an expedition to the lakes of northern Wisconsin promises a connection with the aura of the Northwoods. Here, the whoosh of an unfurling forward cast is occasionally drowned out by the call of a loon, and calming vistas of majestic pine and birch forests are occasionally disturbed by the sudden appearance of a submarine-like apparition following your fly.

The Addictive Allure of the Steelhead's Tug

PORTLAND, OREGON—COME SEPTEMBER, MANY MEMBERS OF PORTland, Oregon's fly-fishing community find themselves heading 100-odd miles east on Interstate 84 to the Deschutes River. They pass mammoth Bonneville Dam and the wind-sport mecca of Hood River, and leave the highway at the town of The Dalles, where a large railroad tie–treating facility abuts the highway. The pungent smell of creosote soon mixes with the sage of the high desert and a heightened sense of anticipation as they near the river. The summer steelhead run is reaching its apex, and few fish evoke such a rabid, near obsessive passion among devotees.

Few are more devoted than Dave Moskowitz.

Moskowitz, an environmental lawyer by training, first fished for steelhead—an ocean-going form of rainbow trout—on the Deschutes in 1987. "I was invited by some of my housemates to accompany them on their annual Deschutes fishing trip," he recalled. "Most fished for trout, but one guy convinced me to go for steelhead. He said to cast across the current and let the fly swing to shore, then take two steps and do it again. He fished below me and I tried to mimic his technique. There was a cry and I looked up to see his rod above his head, and a huge bright silver fish cartwheeling downstream. He and the fish soon parted ways. I looked at the water around me and took several steps back—fearful of fish that large swimming around my legs."

Moskowitz was intrigued. But it would be five more years of intermittent angling before he brought his first steelhead to hand.

There's a saying among steelhead aficionados that goes "the tug is the drug"; that is, the excitement of the steelhead's take keeps anglers coming back. There's no question that there's a visceral thrill when a fish grabs the fly—the reel screams madly as line spins off, and the fish leaps madly, leaving the angler holding on for dear life and praying that all her knots will hold.

But perhaps more addictive than the take is the *hope* that the fish will grab the fly . . . or that the fish are even present. Steelhead spend their early years in the river, and then migrate to the sea. After a year or more of intensive feeding, they return to their natal river to spawn, weighing from five to 20 pounds . . . and on some rivers, more. Steelhead begin showing up in the Deschutes in late June, with new fish entering the river through October. Unlike trout feeding on dry flies or rolling tarpon, steelhead seldom show themselves. You enter a run or pool hoping some fish might be holding there. To make matters worse, steelhead seldom eat once they're in the river; they seem to take a fly as an act of aggression. Even if they're present where you're fishing, they have to be in the mood—presumably a *bad* mood—to bite.

For all these reasons, fishing for steelhead is one of angling's great acts of faith. Steelheaders may log long days of fishing in cold and rainy conditions—and thousands of casts—with nary a bite. But something goads them on.

In the 26 years since his first encounter, Moskowitz has learned a good deal about the habits of Deschutes steelhead, and how to catch them. He spends 40 to 50 days on the river each season and knows all the famous runs intimately—Lockit, Hot Rocks, Magic, Greenlight, Wagonblast—as well as countless little spots that most overlook. He's a competent fly tier, favoring dry flies like the Strung-Out Skater; and while not the river's longest caster, he throws a spey rod well enough to cover the water. Professional guides and river regulars know him as a consummate gentleman, ever willing to share a run, an effective fly, or a cold beer.

Moskowitz has two children and an overall well-rounded life. But he's the first to admit that come late June, he's "the most evasive, noncommittal guy around. Steelheading has definitely led me to give up on some relationships with women. I know myself well, and I'm up front with people about what I like to do."

Moskowitz has also been a dogged champion of the river and its fish, working for a variety of conservation organizations over the years. "Dave has passion for fishing and for the fish, and recognizes the two passions are inseparable," said Bill Bakke, Science and Conservation Director for Native Fish Society, which advocates for the recovery and preservation of native fish species. "His enthusiasm for the Deschutes is infectious, and he's brought many people into the conservation community. The Pacific Northwest is better for his efforts, though many anglers may not know it."

Moskowitz's most recent endeavor is The Deschutes River Alliance, a nonprofit that aims to protect the water quality and fish habitat of the river.

On a Friday afternoon in late September, I accompanied Moskowitz to a section of the Deschutes called Kloan, seven miles from the river's confluence with the Columbia. A precariously steep and narrow dirt road leads to a small parking area. Weathered remnants of a handmade sign hang by the path leading to the river. It used to read, "Life Starts Here." Fall rains had arrived early, cloaking the canyon in shades of gray. Moskowitz led me from run to run suggesting where the fish were most likely to be resting—and always letting me cast over the most promising water. At a spot called Signal Light, I watched my line swing across the water as the gray began to give way to black. Near the end of the swing, there was a sharp tug on my line. Instinctively, I lifted the rod . . . exactly the wrong thing to do. The fish was gone, and that was the only tug of the outing.

Heading back to Portland, we stopped in Hood River for an IPA at Double Mountain Brewery, a favorite post-fishing watering hole. I began to bewail my lost opportunity, but Moskowitz offered solace. "A few years back, I lost 18 fish in a row. Another year, 13. It happens."

Mojitos, Muchachas, y Sábalo

Thanks to an agreement between an Italian company (Avalon) that's based in Argentina and the government of Cuba, anglers have had the privilege of fishing Los Jardines de la Reina (The Gardens of the Queen) for the last 18 years. Tales of Los Jardines' unblemished and underexploited waters—plus the forbidden-fruit appeal of Cuba—have made the archipelago a much sought-after flats destination . . . especially in the spring, when migrating adult tarpon begin passing through.

This past April, I was invited to join a small group of writers (assembled by Jim Klug of Yellow Dog Flyfishing Adventures) to visit Los Jardines and Isla de la Juventud (Island of the Youth). Avalon's interest in hosting our party was (presumably) to rekindle American interest in Cuba as a fly-fishing destination, especially as there are some signs that the embargo barring casual travel may be nearing its conclusion. My interest in attending—beyond many friends' entreaties that "you've got to go before it opens up to Americans and becomes like Disneyland"—was the opportunity to cast to, hook, jump, and land my first adult tarpon. I'd fished for baby tarpon in the Yucatán, and my interest had been piqued. Watching a 20-pound fish leap three feet into the air, scales gleaming, was exciting. I couldn't quite imagine the thrill of a fish three, four, or eight times the size of my Yucatán fish breaking the surface, attached to my fly.

I signed on.

Though my journalist visa was denied (the purpose of my trip was interpreted as encouraging visitation and commercial activity with Cuba), I plodded on, flying below the radar via Mexico to what would certainly be an adventure . . . and to what I was fairly certain would be 70 or 80 pounds of tarpon flesh pressed against mine.

Tarpon Time

Like most Caribbean flats destinations, Los Jardines' fishery highlights bonefish, permit, tarpon (baby and adult), and snook, with jacks and barracuda an ever-available distraction. During my early April visit, the adult tarpon had just begun arriving as they made their way north toward spawning grounds in the Gulf of Mexico, and the guides were in the throes of *sábalo* mania. Though we poled around some flats on the ocean side of Los Jardines and found a few juvenile fish in the 15- to 25-pound range, most of the tarpon efforts were focused in Boca Grande, a wide channel about 40 minutes' run to the west of La Tortuga. I learned on the trip to Boca (which we took three out of our six angling days) that Dolphins are not the ideal craft for long open-water runs—especially across the boca itself. Toward the end of my week, I found myself sizing up the diving guests and crew members for their potential as kidney donors, as I was fairly certain mine were about to give out thanks to the constant battering of the waves against the bow.

Upon reaching the west side of Boca Grande, our guides staked up the Dolphins at 200-yard intervals. To the right was a white sand flat, roughly three feet deep; to the left, a deeper channel. With one angler standing in front, one seated in the middle (alternating between minding the casting angler's line and drinking Cristal), and the guide on the poling platform, we scanned the waters to the south and waited for the fish. Sometimes the wait was 40 minutes, sometimes two hours; on one occasion we waited until lunchtime, and the fish never showed.

But on the occasions they did, it was game on.

Every time.

Though it was not a game I played well on this, my first adult tarpon adventure.

A good friend who regularly chases tarpon in Key West and Homosassa had told me how finicky/spooky/indifferent the fish can be. "You might see 100 fish in a day's fishing out of Homosassa, but they won't eat," he warned. This was on my mind the first morning on Boca Grande when our guide, Leonardo Arche, cried, "They're coming!" Seventy-five yards in front of the boat, a dozen silhouettes appeared. By their size and shape, there was no question that they were tarpon. I was on deck, and after a few false casts I dropped a chartreuse 3/0 Toad a few yards in front and to the left of the fish, now 25 yards away. One strip, and two fish peeled away from the school. A second strip, and the basketball-size mouth of one of the fish closed over the fly. "Set!" Arche yelled, and I pulled back hard on the line. The fish—somewhere between 75 and 85 pounds, we estimated—catapulted into the air. Watching in wonder as the sun sparkled against the fish's scales, I neglected to bow the rod to provide a bit of slack before the fish crashed back in the water.

And the fish was gone.

This set the tone for my tarpon experiences the remainder of the trip. At Jardines, fish would approach the boat in waves, sometimes five tarpon, sometimes a dozen, a few times upwards of 20. If the fly was placed anywhere in their field of vision, the fish were almost unfailingly game to take . . . and this angler was equally steadfast in his inability to close the deal.

For most species I've pursued, getting the fish to take is 90 percent of the battle. There may be a few long runs and other moments of truth (a snag across the river, a rapid downstream, a knot in the backing). With tarpon, it seems, making the cast and getting the take is only the beginning. Once the fish has grabbed the fly, time seems to accelerate at an exponential pace, as does the potential for things to go wrong. The line that you've stripped in around your feet speeds back through the guides of the rod, providing ample opportunities to tangle around a zinger, your shirt button, your reel, the fighting butt of the rod or your toes; I parted ways with fish each of these ways. Fail to put enough pressure on the line and the hook won't set securely in the tarpon's tough jaw (two fish lost this way); put too much pressure and you can pop the leader or cause the rod sections to come apart (two more fish lost this way).

While I came up empty, almost all of the other anglers (including several first-time *tarponistas*) found success. The general consensus: If you can avoid the miscues outlined above and survive the first 30 seconds of pandemonium, you have a pretty good chance of landing your tarpon.

And if you're fishing in Jardines when the tarpon are running, you're going to get enough shots to make the frequently cited "land one of ten hooked" statistic work for you.

Between waves of fish, there was lots of time to consider my failings as a tarpon angler. None of my technical shortcomings—clearing line, bowing the rod, maintaining the right degree of pressure—were that difficult to overcome. Some of these deficiencies might subside over time as I gained what might be termed "muscle memory." The problem that would be more difficult to transcend was also more difficult to confront—a lack of grace under pressure. Most of us want to think that we'd respond well in a situation that required quick, decisive action. I was left thinking that if I couldn't respond effectively to a damn fish—how would I respond if someone snatched one of my girls at a county fair, or if my brakes went out coming around Mount Hood with my boat trailer?

To distract myself from such a morose topic, I tried to engage our guides with my very broken Spanish. A number of sociopolitical themes consistently emerged:

- Being a fly-fishing guide is a very good job to have in Cuba.
- Though Fidel and Raul will probably die soon, another family member or someone from the inner circle will take over.
- Little will change in Cuba for a long time, whoever is in power.
- Cuban people bear no ill will to Americans, despite all propaganda to the contrary.
- Many Cuban men maintain several girlfriends in addition to their wives and children, and are happy to discuss said girlfriends' amorous proclivities.
- It was at these times I was glad that our language barrier prohibited more nuanced discussions.

If tarpon were the focus of our angling exploits, bonefish were a much appreciated diversion. On the days we crossed Boca Grande, we'd stop and fish an ocean-side flat or two en route as we waited for the tide to shift. These same flats provided a consolation prize on the way back after a morning of losing tarpon. Each time we hit a bonefish flat, we were into schools of fish within 10 minutes of lifting the motor. One of my angling companions, Charlie Levine, was new to fly fishing and bonefish, and he had hourlong stretches where he landed 10 fish. Accuracy-challenged casts were not showstoppers; the fish would scatter momentarily and reunite seconds later, ready to eat Gotchas, Crazy Charlies, and just about any other smallish tan fly presented. I recall only a few occasions where our boat managed to spook a school out of reach. More often, the schools were pushed along by marauding barracuda or jacks, or we grew restless and moved on to find a fresh school or to visit the tarpon. The bones were bigger than I anticipated, averaging around three pounds, with my largest to hand about five. Several fish pushing the 10-pound mark were landed by other anglers on the trip.

I'd always heard that jacks were extremely fast, though I'd never had firsthand experience. It's true—they are a blue flash across the flats, like a shooting star. During one bonefish session, a pack screamed by. Our guide Leonardo yelled, "Get the spinning rod!" I opted for the 12-weight. When the pack zipped by again, I flipped a big popper 30 feet out. One twitch, and three jacks were vying for it. The biggest in the group (about 15 pounds) won and seconds later it was 100 yards off the flat—pure, simple visceral fun, with little chance for failure.

It flashed through my mind that perhaps we'd be better served by bailing on the boca and the tarpon and instead focusing on the jacks. True, they didn't jump. But they pulled hard and took flies on top, and once they were on, they were on. Jacks seemed the whitefish of the flats—an afterthought (and even poor substitute) for the tarpon/trout as far as the cognoscenti were concerned, but a vigorous tug that's more attainable (and more or less the same experience) for the uninitiated.

On to Island of the Youth

Isla de la Juventud rests roughly 90 miles south of Havana. Once Isla de Pinos (Island of Pines), its name was changed after the revolution when young comrades from the mainland and beyond were brought there for indoctrination in the ways of socialism. The island's most significant settlement is Nueva Gerona (population 25,000, give or take), and that's where our group was based for the second fishing leg of our adventure. There's ferry service from Havana, but flying is a bit faster . . . though I'd rank it as the least comfortable flight of my life, even though it was less than 40 minutes. The butterscotch candy we each received upon stepping on to the plane came, I would soon learn, in lieu of water, air conditioning, or any laminar air flow whatsoever. The Cyrillic script on the plane's bulkhead spoke to its Russian homeland. Had I not sweated through my shirt and stuck to my seat in the 100-plus-degree heat, I would've been able to look out the window to see the plane's badly bald tires. Though passengers did not receive a second butterscotch, each of us were provided with a complimentary copy of *Granma International*, the official broadsheet of Cuba. It included a daily reflection from Fidel.

The harrowing puddle jump to Nueva Gerona proved a preamble to one of the trip's most wonderful moments. Stepping out of the cab at Hotel Rancho El Tesoro, I spied five young men smiling shyly, standing by a small table in the hotel's open lobby where ingredients for mojitos were set out. Soon the men picked up instruments—two guitars, a hand drum, stand-up bass, maracas—and launched into song. They were smiling, ebullient, thrilled to have someone to play for. And they did play well, the instrumentalists answering the handsome, shuffling lead singer in four-part harmony as they made their way through a few numbers from the Great Cuban Songbook, as well as some original songs.

I've played guitar with a modest level of proficiency for almost 30 years, have played in three or four bands and have loved music as long as I can remember. (In the spirit of full disclosure: I did see the Grateful Dead 40-plus times before Jerry's demise.) These days, music provides a welcome respite from reason and analysis. For me, playing is about feeling. With these five young musicians, I connected through that shared feeling. Yes, this musical greeting was a set piece orchestrated for our consumption, yet it was perhaps the most heartfelt interaction of the trip, as these young men seemed to play for the joy of playing. It was made only better by the band inviting me to join in . . . and graciously enduring my at times atonal contributions on my Backpacker guitar. (I later left the guitar with these lads, as instruments—like everything else—are hard to come by in Cuba.)

By the way—if you want to curry favor with musicians in Cuba, ask them to play "Hotel California." Every band seems to know it.

Reaching the fishing grounds of the Archipelago de los Canarreos from Nueva Gerona required a 20-minute van ride to Avalon's makeshift marina on the banks of the Jucaro River, and then a minimum 40-minute run in a Dolphin. The wind was blowing a solid 20 knots on our first two days, renewing the onslaught on our collective kidneys. Thanks to the wind (which kept us off the water one day) and the fact that the tarpon had just begun arriving, we spent much of our time blind-casting to likely lies and channels with sinking-tip lines. A number of fish were hooked and landed this way, though it's not quite like sight-casting to cruisers. However, as a guide friend in Texas once said, "I'll take any tarpon in the air!"

It was not all this way. On the second to last day in Nueva Gerona, our guide Maikel confided, "I have a secret spot. Many big tarpon!" After poling around an open lagoon and landing a few bonefish, Maikel pointed to a narrow channel back in the mangroves—"They're here." Even from 300 yards away, we could see dorsal fins breaking the water, a dozen or so tarpon porpoising . . . in fact, looking much like porpoises. As we edged into the mangroves, Matt Hansen took the bow. Out of the breeze, the already warm air became sultry, and the bugs that had been almost completely absent the entire trip intensified. Letting the bugs settle on his brow, Matt cast as we edged closer to the still-happy fish. When we were 60 feet from the pod, a fish blurped and Matt dropped a cast into the widening circles of its riseform. Two strips and his line came tight, and the fish was airborne, once, twice, three times. Maikel slowly poled the boat out of the mangroves in case the fish decided to run, instructing Matt to keep the rod tip down, that this would keep the fish from heading into the mangroves and an inevitable parting. It worked. Fifteen minutes later, I snapped a photo of Matt and his tarpon—around 75 pounds—on the bow. This was Matt's first adult tarpon to hand.

I was truly happy to see Matt land his fish. Borrowing his camera (a much higher-quality model than my own), I had documented the whole process, and I was proud of my shots. Caught up in the general spirit of success that enveloped the boat, I briefly convinced myself that I enjoyed watching Matt catch his fish as much as if I had caught it myself. Of course, I hoped this gesture of karmic goodwill and generosity of spirit would result in the tarpon gods smiling down upon me. They did, in a manner of speaking. Pushing back into the lagoon, several fish blurped before us. On my first cast, a fish slashed at the fly but missed. When a fish rolled behind the boat, I flipped a backcast in its direction. At that moment, two other fish rolled 30 feet in front of me. As I started to lift the line to drop the fly on them, the line came tight, and a fish was in the air. You can imagine how this ended. The tarpon gods had punished me twofold—once indignity for my incompetence, once for my duplicity.

NOTE: By all reports, fishing in later spring can be off the charts. A friend of mine and his wife jumped more than 130 adult tarpon in one week two Junes ago; one of the guides substantiated this claim unprompted.

Riding around Nuevo Gerona, scenes of bucolic (if somewhat scraggly) agrarian life were juxtaposed with the bizarre. Just past a farm where more of Cuba's emaciated livestock foraged near the roadside, a large, featureless concrete building rose four or five stories. As best as I could surmise, it was one of the dorms for "the youth." We later came upon others. Some seemed to have residents (squatters?); others looked empty. These structures, little tidbits of Soviet Eastern Bloc architecture, seemed as if they'd been airlifted to the middle of the Caribbean from Romania or East Germany, and fit in as well as tarpon would in the Ural River. On the day we were blown off the water, we visited Presidio Modelo, a penitentiary that was erected in the mid-1920s and housed convicts and later political prisoners. The facility's five circular structures resemble small sporting arenas, though the 6-by-9-foot cells (for two men) could not have been very comfortable for viewing the melees that ensued when prisoners were allowed to roam free within the structure. The strange thing: though Presidio Modelo is Cuba's equivalent to Alcatraz, no attendants were present, and we were free to roam around as we wished.

Back to Havana

Our first night in Havana, we found ourselves standing in Plaza de la Catedral (Cathedral Square) in Old Havana, receiving what might have been construed as either a warning or a pep talk from Jim Klug. "You don't have to go to Casa de la Musica, but I think it's part of the Havana experience. But be prepared. There are lots of beautiful women there, but they're extremely aggressive and persistent. They will grab your junk as you walk by, and try to get you to dance. Then they'll try to get you to go off with them—but understand that they're working. Whatever you do, don't accept a drink from anyone, or even leave your drink unattended. A guy who was here last year drank a beer someone offered him and woke up in a speeding cab between two women. He fought his way past one woman and rolled out of the moving cab, and showed up at the Parque Central as the bus to Jucaro was ready to pull away. He slept for the bus ride, the boat ride, and the first three days on Tortuga. This was no wild man—he's an accountant from the Midwest."

Scores of cars—many of 1950s vintage, a fulfillment of many a Havana travelogue—were parked pell-mell in front of La Casa, a nightclub in the midst of a residential neighborhood. Among the cars were men peddling what I assumed were drugs, women, cigarettes, rides—whatever was available—though with only a smattering of Spanish at my disposal, I wasn't certain. They had the aggressive entrepreneurial spirit I associate with pimps. Inside, the scene was much as Jim had described, a cauldron of beautiful women in many hues (reflecting generations of Euro/Afro/Indian intermingling), some seated at tables, some parked by passageways, as if in ambush. As we made our way across the floor to a glassed-in bar Jim had identified as a "safe zone" (less frequented by the club's more aggressive ladies), our man parts were indeed grabbed, and propositions were indeed made. A phalanx of young women entered the fishbowl area as we sipped Cristals (the rather characterless lager that along with its malt liquor cousin Bucanero makes up the beer offering of Cuba), nuzzling up to the man at the far end of the bar (if he looked like an American or European) and asking him to dance, or offering a casual observation like "I'm very good at sex." If rebuffed, their faces showed a mix of bewilderment (you're turning *this* down at the cost of a decent bottle of wine?) and determination as they moved down the line to chat up the next fellow.

Looking back on that evening, I've tried to find some metaphor for Havana, Cuba, and our fishing experience:

- In the turbulent, developing world, tables turn quickly, and the fisherman can suddenly become the quarry.
- In a land of paucity, everyone must fish to get ahead.

In the end, the evening inspired the first verse of a song:

No es sábalo en la Casa de la Musica
Though the spirits flow like tides across the flats
You can cast your line far out across the dance floor
But all you'll ever catch is just the crabs

I'm in the minority when I say that I was not especially taken by Havana. In some poor/developing countries, one has a sense of a slow but forward-moving struggle toward stability and a better life for the people; in Havana (and Cuba overall), there's a sense of slow decay instead of progress. It's evident in the darkness enveloping a city of several million when approached from its outskirts early on a Friday evening, in the many once-grand buildings now slowly crumbling, in the listlessness of large segments of the populous who seemed to be waiting for something—jobs, tourists, a parade? Those who were not waiting were hustling what little there was to be hustled—women, cigars, a recommendation for a good restaurant (restaurateurs are expected to give hustlers a "commission" for any customers they bring in). It cannot be helped that most of our interactions with the Cuban people began as set pieces, as our group did not exactly blend in with the locals. There's the lady with the big cigar near Cathedral Square that you can pose with for a picture for a few convertible pesos (more commonly called CUCs); there's the guy who wants to show you the *real* Hemingway bar, or introduce you to his cousin; there are the throngs of pedicab drivers with bikes ingeniously fabricated from discarded rebar jockeying for a fare; there's the guy shilling his paintings of Che Guevara graffiti; there are stilt dancers and their brass band accompanists in the squares. They all exist more or less for your consumption as a visitor, like the silver-painted robot dancers on Bourbon Street and Fisherman's Wharf. Were the denizens of Havana *only* interested in our money? No. Some would linger to chat (as much as the language barrier allowed) after their hustle was rebuffed. Like the guides, they seemed to harbor no animosity toward *Americanos*, nor any fealty to the Castro regime. They have a meager roof over their heads and (just barely) enough to eat, but not much more.

Despite the bright colors, the occasional music (not as prevalent as the film *Buena Vista Social Club* would suggest), and the many bars that Hemingway frequented (there's some variance in each bar's mojito recipe, usually indicated by the quantity of muddled mint), the sense of resignation I felt hovering over Havana made it mildly depressing. That being said, it's worth a visit, if only for a day. And if you have an extra morning or afternoon, do go to the Hemingway house outside town. You can't go inside, but staring in through the windows at the bookshelves filled with first editions as you circle the domicile, things seem untouched since Papa's last visit. Rumor has it that if you slip the woman standing guard over Hemingway's writing desk in the lighthouse-like tower below the house 10 CUCs, she'll snap a picture of you at said desk. She may be the richest woman in Cuba.

The most curious Cuban comment during our visit: a used bookseller in the flea market square in Old Havana whose stall displayed at least 30 different books on Che called after us to "Give my regards to Bryan Adams."

I didn't have the heart to explain that he's Canadian.

Lobstermen Turn to Guiding in the Yucatán

PUNTA ALLEN, Mexico—For nearly two millennia, the Mayan people along the Yucatán Peninsula's Caribbean coast have relied on fishing for both sustenance and trade. The tradition continues, though today many Mayan fishermen are as likely to be throwing a 10-weight graphite fly rod as a net.

With the Yucatán's emergence as a popular flats-fishing destination, local lobstermen have been recruited as fly-fishing guides to lead anglers to bonefish, tarpon, and permit.

"At some saltwater destinations, it's not uncommon for guides from the Florida Keys to be airlifted in to lead guests to fish," said Dick Cameron, owner of the Palometa Club, a fly-fishing lodge in Punta Allen, a village at the end of the Boca Paila peninsula, 30 miles from Tulum, that specializes in permit (*palometa*). "It's been different on Ascension Bay. Jan Isley, a renowned Keys guide who discovered the region's fly-fishing possibilities in the '80s, also recognized the potential the local lobstermen had as guides. He understood that these men are out on the water all the time, and know where the fish are."

Through a happy coincidence, the spiny lobster–fishing season runs from July through February . . . and the prime sport-fishing season on Ascension Bay runs from March through June. Lodge owners like Cameron have selectively recruited guides from the local lobster-fishing cooperative—Mexican Pescadores de Vigía Chico Cooperative—for over 20 years.

"There are three good jobs you can find in Punta Allen," said Gerardo Velasquez, one of Palometa Club's staff of 14 guides. "Lobster fishing, eco-guiding, and guiding fly fishermen. Guiding fishermen pays better than guiding eco-tourists, and it's fun. I'd say that lobster fishing is easier than guiding, especially if you're trying to catch permit. To be a good permit guide, you need lots of passion and patience. It's a hard game."

Punta Allen has less than 500 residents. Velasquez estimates that 60 to 70 men in town guide anglers for at least part of the fishing season.

Lobster fishing in Ascension Bay bears little resemblance to the occupation as it's practiced off the Maine coast. Fishermen place small "houses" at depths from two to 60 feet. The houses provide shelter on the sandy expanses of the bay, attracting lobsters. Fishermen free dive to collect lobsters that have gathered in the houses. Cooperative rules dictate that undersize and female lobsters are returned to the water. "I grew up around commercial fishing in Alaska," Cameron added, "and in my experience, commercial activities don't tend to complement sport-fishing efforts. It's been the opposite here. As the commercial fishery has thrived, there have been more little lobsters around, and that means more food for the bonefish and permit."

On a bright March morning, I accompanied Raza Tallim, an angler from Calgary, Alberta, and guides Julio Octavio Gamboa and Charlie Rendon for a day of fishing. The water was an ever-shifting palette of blues and greens as we motored across Ascension Bay in a 23-foot *panga*, the de facto fishing craft for these parts. Tallim hoped to catch a snook, as he'd landed his first tarpon and permit during the previous days' fishing. We reached some stands of mangroves at the southern end of the bay, ideal snook habitat. Rendon climbed to the poling platform and Gamboa went to the bow with Tallim. As Rendon poled the panga around the mangroves, he shared how he came to guiding. "I knew nothing about fly fishing when I started 17 years ago. A friend asked me to take some guys out to where the fish are. I did so. The guys had a good time, and they asked me to take them another day. I did this for a month and was offered a job guiding. A friend taught me how to cast in his yard. I was given an old fiberglass rod, and eventually bought my own graphite rod."

Near some mangroves populated by a noisy flock of pink spoonbills and white ibis, Gamboa spotted a snook. He instructed Tallim to cast his fly into a pocket among the branches where the fish was resting, but Tallim's casts were a bit high and landed in the mangroves. Rendon stepped down and demonstrated a sidearm technique. Tallim was a quick study and slid his next cast under the branches, but the fish was gone.

After lunch, Rendon motored to a large flat of slightly deeper water. "We saw big schools of permit here yesterday," he said. As he killed the motor and began poling the boat, Gamboa changed Tallim's fly to a crab pattern. "Permit!" Rendon cried suddenly. The mood on the boat became serious. Rendon called out rapid instructions in Spanish to Gamboa in the bow: "*Izquierdo* [left]! *Mas derecho* [more right]!" Gamboa interpreted them for Tallim. "Cast 10 o'clock, 40 feet," he said softly. Tallim made the cast, perhaps a bit long. Several ghostlike shadows [the permit] flew past the boat, and a larger shadow [a shark] lumbered slowly away. "I was casting to the shark; I thought it was the permit," Tallim said dejectedly. "It's okay," Rendon reassured him.

As the afternoon wore on, the wind came up. We fished the flat a few more times. Each drift through, a few permit appeared. The guide team positioned Tallim to make casts, but there were no takers. Tallim, like most sage permit anglers, was philosophical: "We didn't get any today, but I learned so much. The casting and fly-retrieving tips I got from Charlie and Julio are worth more than getting a fish."

How to Get Skunked on the Bulkley and Threaten Your Marriage at the Same Time

Having recently moved to Oregon and been bitten by the steelhead bug—and having a friend in the fishing travel business who regaled me with tales of the chrome monsters lurking in the famed Bulkley—I decided to make the trek north. A spendy B.C. lodge was out of the question on my budget, but a tent wouldn't do either, as my wife and 18-month-old daughter (and the wife and two young children of my fishing companion, Peter) would be in tow. The same friend had assured us that the Bulkley's hub town—Smithers—would be great fun for the families, and that the most comfortable and economical way to do the trip would be to rent a house on the river that was owned by an area lodge operator . . . and that there was lots of access for do-it-yourselfers.

It should be noted here that said friend stayed at a spendy lodge, had no children at the time, has a wife who's an excellent angler, and fished with guides. I knew all this at the time, but was careful to not let such knowledge interfere with my bad judgment.

We started our trek north with a two-day stopover in Vancouver, a delightful cosmopolitan city; our brief habitation here was by far the smartest thing Peter and I managed in our plan. (The second smartest was an overnight here on the sojourn south.) Early on the third morning, with memories of our ambles in Stanley Park still fresh in mind, we began the 12-hour drive north in Pete's new Honda Odyssey; the families would fly up that evening (the only other smart facet of our plan). As we left the suburbs, an LED sign on the highway warned us to "Beware of Wildlifes." We chortled at the misplaced plural, though did not discount the possibility that the grizzlies, elk, wolves, etc., would be so plentiful that the *s* might be justified. We passed through towns surprisingly devoid of charm—Williams Lake, Quesnel, Prince George—marking our progress with coffee/meal stops at Tim Hortons (a cross between Dunkin Donuts and Dennys, and a culinary mainstay in this part of the world). After Prince George, we veered northwest for the last 150 miles (or so) of our journey. As the last light leaked from the sky near Vanderhoof, the clouds gave way to light rain. By Houston, with its statue of the world's largest fly rod, the rain was falling in earnest. We couldn't make out the shade of the little Bulkley near its junction with the Morice (a much larger river; by all rights the Bulkley should be called the Morice) in the darkness. This, in retrospect, was a small blessing, as we had at least one night of hopeful steelhead dreams.

When we woke the next morning, the rain had mostly stopped, but the damage had been done—the Bulkley flowed a dismal gray, like washing machine outflow after a very dirty load of laundry. We decided a trip to town was in order to show our families its many child-friendly amenities, and to get a bit of local angling knowledge. We soon learned that Smithers was undergoing a major public works project—the main artery had been scraped down to the dirt, traffic was reduced to one lane, and many adjoining sidewalks were blocked with large sewer pipes. Traversing the pipes, we eventually found a sporting goods store with a fly-fishing section. When I asked a store employee which dry fly he liked to use on the Bulkley—after all, it was famed for its surface-seeking steelhead—he seemed to staunch a guffaw and pointed instead to an assortment of long black leeches . . . the kind of thing we'd use at home in the winter. When I asked about access, he asked if we had guides, and when I said no, he said it was pretty limited, and pointed out a few spots on a map he sold us. "Most of the guys on their own put in and float," he added. "You guys have boats?"

They were safe at home.

But Gunter, our host, did have a few pontoon boats that he was happy to rent us for the week, and the fee was just a little more than buying a boat of our own. Gunter was a curious character, a burly Austrian who closely resembled my vision of a "burgher" except instead of wearing lederhosen, he favored a T-shirt promoting his lodge that he wore every day and that didn't quite cover his rotund tummy. He was obviously a festive soul, as a banner reading "Happy Birthday Helga" still hung in the house's mudroom off the garage. It turned out that the grounds of our rental home were the nerve center of what he called his "Mobile Unit"—an RV/boat combination that allowed him to take salmon-seeking clients where the action was on the Lower Skeena and beyond. Gunter was officious in his manner, and suspect of his clients' angling ability. "I had three guys from Norway on the Skeena salmon fishing," he explained shortly after our first meeting. "They said, 'There are no fish here.' I grabbed the rod and cast out and caught a 30-pounder, one cast." So there. Once we had our boats, we had to figure out how to get them down to the river, as the bank was quite steep. Given Gunter's general ambivalence toward guest fishermen, I wagered Peter a beer that if we asked him how to get the boats down, he would tell us to jump in them and slide down.

"How do you get the boats down to the river?"

"Get in and slide down!"

As we were roping them down the cliff, he added, "Fish the bends!"

For the next five days, we fished the bends, the riffles, and the runs of the eight or so miles between Gunter's house and the highway bridge just east of downtown—the last take-out before the canyon section of the Bulkley, home, we learned later, to many of the river's most famous runs, and pretty much out of the question for day-trippers on their own. As the week passed, the water cleared a wee bit, going from the dirty laundry outflow shade to the color of glacial till. Part of the problem, we realized, was the abundance of pink salmon flesh in the system. After every third swing of our leeches, it was necessary to clean the hook of salmon gook. And if we weren't hooking fish matter, we were getting tangled up with the millions of cottonwood leaves drifting toward Mother Skeena. Beyond flesh, flotsam, and one small bull trout, we found nothing. Not a tug.

By our third day of floating what we came to think of as our "home water," we began to see a few other anglers flogging away. They shared that a few of the other venerable Skeena tributaries—the Copper, the Kispiox, and the Babine—were running fairly clear, and people were finding a few fish. Had we considered going over there? "Over there" meant a few hours' drive—no problem for Peter and I, who were used to driving a few hours each way to the Deschutes for half a day's fishing. But four extra hours of driving meant four *more* hours away from our families.

Oh yes—our families.

Each early evening when we returned to the house above the Bulkley, our wives greeted us with eyes that shone with a mix of derision and desperation—the former, a function of our fine plan to strand them some eight miles south of nowhere; the latter, a direct correlation to being stranded with three toddlers, very few toys, and no town diversions beyond a public pool/water park with limited family hours and the pleasure of dropping off our shuttle vehicle—an ancient pickup truck whose use came with the house—at the aforementioned bridge. Had there been somewhere to go, I have no doubt our saintly spouses would've thrust the children into our casting-sore arms and gone. As there wasn't, they merely opened a bottle of wine and glowered at us across the table, expressing little sympathy for the off-color water, the salmon gook, and the opportunity denied of driving to the Babine, Copper, etc. . . . though in the spirit of full disclosure, I should say that neither Peter nor I had the guts to even float the "driving to other rivers" notion, given the current circumstances.

It's worth noting that in the seven years since our fateful trip to Smithers, my wife has not once expressed an interest in returning. In fact, I don't believe that she's ever mentioned it.

On our fourth day of flogging, it happened. We were at a promising-looking riffle about midway through the float. I took a spot near the head, and Peter positioned himself 100 yards downstream. I flipped a purple leech about 30 feet out, and midway through the swing came THE PULL. I yelped and backed up onto the gravel bar to dig in for what would certainly be an epic struggle—me versus the iconic Bulkley steelhead. I waited for line to scream from the reel, but it didn't so much as murmur. The fish was still there, just not doing a damn thing. I began reeling and it dutifully swam in. With 10 feet of line outside the rod tip, the fish came in view—it was seven or eight pounds, moderately bright, nothing remarkable. At this point, it didn't begin to fight so much as thrash about, shaking its head.

Before Peter could scramble up the bar to see this marvel, our first B.C. steelhead, it shook itself free and drifted back into the murk. Few events in my fishing life have been so anticlimactic.

The next day—our last on the river—Peter took the slot at the head of the very same riffle, flipped a purple leech out and yelped. Another hookup! After waiting for a searing run that was never to come, Pete reeled the fish in, saw that it was about eight pounds, and parted company with it not far from his feet when the fish began shaking its head.

To this day, I'm convinced that it was the same fish, for all I know, the only steelhead that entered the Bulkley in the fall of 2001.

Makos on the Fly

SAN DIEGO—The green fairways of Torrey Pines Golf Course were visible through a veil of marine fog as our 24-foot skiff rolled on gentle swells a mile or so offshore. My reverie of contending in a future U.S. Open on the storied links was broken by my angling companion Geoff Roach's exclamation: "We've got one coming in!" Peering over the starboard gunwale, I spied the dorsal fin and then full profile of a shortfin mako shark. The fish—80 pounds, our guide, Conway Bowman, guessed—swam alongside the skiff, then circled away. Bowman cast a teaser bait—an orange rubber squid sans hook—50 feet off the boat and slowly retrieved. The shark reappeared, dorsal fin breaking the surface. "Cast at the teaser!" Bowman called as the shark accelerated. Grabbing a hardy 14-weight fly rod, I slapped a 25-foot cast near the bait. Bowman pulled the teaser away as I stripped the fly. Not 12 feet from the boat, the mako engulfed the fly. I stripped the fly line hard to set the hook in the shark's tough jaw. It shook its head once, twice, as if in disbelief at what was happening, then began screaming line off the reel. Fifty yards away the shark leaped into the air, its nose eight feet above the water. For a moment its blue-black body was suspended parallel above the gray Pacific.

Shortfin mako sharks are distinguished by a less pronounced dorsal fin, a pointy snout, and an orthodontist's nightmare of teeth. Mature fish can reach over 12 feet in length, and weights exceeding 1,200 pounds. The fish are capable of bursts of speed approaching 60 miles per hour. Prized for their incredible leaping ability (makos have been known to clear the water by over 20 feet), the fish have long been a target for anglers using conventional tackle. Historically, makos brought to the boat have often been killed. Given the startling decline in shark populations, many sport fishermen are now practicing catch-and-release fishing. (The practice has been highlighted in the Flying Mako, a catch-and-release fly-fishing tournament dedicated to West Coast pelagic sharks each August off San Diego.)

Though generally found far offshore, the waters bordering San Diego serve as one of the primary breeding grounds for makos. Juvenile fish—animals up to 300 pounds—frequent the inner coastal waters during the summer months, feeding on yellowtail jacks, bonito, and other forage fish. Makos are sometimes encountered disturbingly close to shore; fish have been within a quarter mile of the beach off La Jolla.

The notion of fly fishing for sharks seems like the product of an overactive (and likely distraught) imagination—perhaps a scribbling from Hunter S. Thompson's notebook after a cocktail of espresso and mescaline. For Conway Bowman, it was a matter of geographic convenience. A native San Diegan, Bowman spent summers fly fishing for trout in Idaho with his schoolteacher father. He became hooked on the sport, but found few freshwater opportunities near home. "In the early nineties, I discovered saltwater fly fishing, and soon learned that sharks were among the most plentiful sport fish off the coast of Southern California," Bowman said. "I bought a 17-foot aluminum boat and began pursuing *them.* After catching 25 blue sharks on my first day out with a fly rod, I realized I was on to something. It took me two years longer to figure out how to get mako sharks to take the fly. Nowadays, if I can draw a mako near the boat, we're almost certain to hook them."

Suffice it to say, fly fishing for mako sharks is not a dainty game. In addition to the telephone pole of a fly rod, reels are outfitted with 800 yards of backing, a stainless steel leader, and footlong blaze-orange flies tied on 8/0 hooks. On an average day, Bowman will motor a few miles offshore to a spot where a current moves through. The current will broadcast a chum slick, which draws sharks close through its olfactory appeal. Our chum was an unappetizing stew of yellowtail carcasses, seasoned with a few tablespoons of menhaden oil. Once the chum bucket is over the side of the boat, the engine is cut and the waiting begins. Sometimes it takes a while for sharks to appear; sometimes their appearance is almost instantaneous. "When you're fishing for makos, the sharks are hunting you, not the other way around," Conway said. "They're not shy; when they turn on, they're like a heat-seeking missile." Casts need not be long nor terrifically accurate; the shark will generally find any fly within a five-foot radius. Once the shark chomps down on the fly, get ready: some fish will take out three or four hundred yards of line in a run. Put another way—you know you're not fighting a 10-inch brook trout!

After fifteen minutes of pitched battle (which left a dark bruise on my hip where I'd leveraged the rod's fighting butt), the fish was alongside the boat. Bowman grabbed the leader with a gloved hand and slid a release device (somewhat like a dentist's tool) down the wire to the barbless fly. With a deft flip of his wrist, the fly popped out, and the shark slowly swam away. With luck, it would one day grow large enough to swim the open waters of its birthright.

Size *Does* Matter When Spey Casting

Steelhead trout, like Atlantic salmon, have been described as "the fish of a thousand casts." On the larger steelhead rivers of the Pacific Northwest and British Columbia—the Skagit and Bulkley among others—hooking a steelhead on a fly may require a thousand very long casts. After all, the longer your cast, the more water you can cover, and the better chance you have of a fish actually seeing your fly.

To achieve consistently long casts over a long day of casting, many Northwest steelhead fly anglers have taken up two-handed rods, and a technique called spey casting. Where traditional single-handed fly casting requires the angler to make a backcast to accelerate the fly line forward, spey casters use the tension of the water to load the rod and make an exaggerated roll cast. The longer spey rod—generally 12 to 16 feet in length—allows the angler to launch the fly 80, 90, or 100 feet. Highly proficient spey casters can toss a fly nearly 200 feet. (The world record spey cast is 295 feet, registered by Steve Rajeff.)

I came to appreciate the advantages of spey casting after a frustrating (and largely fruitless) fall steelhead season on the Lower Deschutes River in north-central Oregon. The Deschutes is powerful and its basalt bottom notoriously slick; there's always the sense that a false step might lead not only to a dunking, but to the big steelhead river in the sky. Discouraged from aggressive wading, I found myself constantly fouled in the tall grasses and/or cottonwoods that extend down to the bank in many spots as I tried to make the 60- or 70-foot casts that would reach the water where the fish were likely lying. On more than one occasion, my fishing buddy Dr. Peter Gyerko hooked fish from runs I had just fished; the 10 or

15 extra feet he could muster made all the difference. Sufficiently emasculated, I sought assistance in the form of a 14-foot spey rod.

Twenty years ago, two-handed rods were almost unheard of in North America, though they were the weapon of choice on Atlantic salmon rivers in the United Kingdom and Scandinavia. The rods' ungainly size was certainly one reason for their lack of adoption here. "When I was introduced to spey casting in the U.K., some anglers were using a rod called the Double-Built Palakona, manufactured by Hardy," said Simon Gawesworth, one of the world's preeminent spey-casting instructors. "It was 18 feet long and weighed 54 ounces—a rod for real men." (Nine-foot single-handed rods weigh in the vicinity of five ounces.) Thanks to advances in graphite fabrication and rod-building technology, my 14-foot rod weighs in at around 10 ounces and cost less than $300. "With the fly lines designed specifically for spey rods now available, I can have most newcomers casting 70 feet with just 15 minutes of instruction," Gawesworth added.

Like any fly casting, throwing a line with a spey rod is not without its frustrations. The gentle sweep of the rod in the hands of Mr. Gawesworth as he forms the "D-Loop" that's central to the cast is effortless; with a forward stroke, his line hisses through the guides. Yet a sweep that's too fast or too slow results in an embarrassing puddle of line. There are even certain perils to spey casting: if you're casting over your right shoulder and forget to anchor your cast on your right side, you can send the fly hurtling at your person at very great speeds. Cases of anglers piercing their waders, their hats, and their flesh with errant casts are not uncommon.

The benefits, however, far outweigh the pitfalls. With the two-handed rod, I can easily make casts far longer than I could ever hope for with my 9-foot rod, and I can do so with less effort—especially with the heavy sinking-tip lines that are necessary to reach fish during the winter months. Just as important, I can control my fly line much better with the two-handed rod, throwing large mends upstream or downstream to slow down or accelerate the fly, depending on the situation. After acquiring my first two-handed rod, I proselytized the benefits of the spey experience to my single-handed brethren, winning several converts—including Dr.

Gyerko, after landing a steelhead behind him on the famed Camp Waters of the North Umpqua.

For spey-casting enthusiasts, the high point on the year's social calendar is the Sandy River Spey Clave, held each May just east of Portland, Oregon. The event was first organized in 2001 by Mark Bachmann, a fly-fishing guide and fly shop owner based in nearby Welches. The two-day festivities (which attract upwards of 1,000 devotees) include how-to seminars conducted by some of the world's leading spey-casting authorities (including George Cook, Dec Hogan, Andy Murray, and Andre Scholz) and the opportunity to demo the latest equipment.

At last year's Spey Clave, knots of anglers chatted as others took turns casting demo rods on the grass of a picnic ground that served as the event's staging area. Nearby, a makeshift kitchen served up free hot dogs and chili. The real action was down on the river, where a procession of presenters demonstrated a host of techniques, from "Snap-Ts" to "Snake Rolls," to hundreds of onlookers. Most bore awestruck expressions as caster after caster easily landed their fly on the opposite bank, some 120 feet away.

The Man Who Brought Trout to a Valley of Gravel

PAGOSA SPRINGS, COLORADO—THE RIO BLANCO TUMBLES OUT OF a range of 12,000-foot mountains in the San Juan National Forest into a picture-perfect valley that's reminiscent of a miniature Yosemite. In its upper reaches, the Blanco runs in a whitewater cascade, where native cutthroat trout thrive. In the valley, on the meadowland of El Rancho Pinoso, a privately owned ranch that rents out cabins and provides fly-fishing access, the water slows and deepens, providing excellent habitat for introduced rainbows that frequently exceed 20 inches.

But it wasn't always that way. Rio Blanco has had a little assistance from a hydrologist named Dave Rosgen.

"When I first visited El Rancho Pinoso in 1987, it seemed like the valley was one big gravel bar," Rosgen said. "The Blanco was anywhere from 350 to 500 feet wide and just inches deep, when the riverbed should be 50 or 60 feet wide. You had a system that had no hope to be anything but a very poor fishery; with a little help, the stream could provide great fish habitat, and give visitors a chance to feel good."

Rosgen began doing stream restoration in the late 1960s, when he worked in the United States Forest Service. There, he witnessed the destruction of streams by the erosion resulting from clear-cutting practices.

"I was upset at the state of the impaired rivers I was seeing," he said. "I wanted to fix them."

In 1984, Rosgen formed Wildland Hydrology, and has been doing watershed assessment and river restoration ever since.

He has worked on hundreds of rivers and streams including Nevada Creek in Montana, the Little Snake River in Wyoming, and the Big Thompson River, the Blue River, and the Rio Blanco in Colorado.

To create a habitat that would support trout in the valley reaches of the Rio Blanco, it was necessary to slow the river enough to stem erosion and create deeper pockets of water to provide shelter for the fish. Before he could begin to create a blueprint to engineer the necessary changes, Rosgen needed to find a river in the region that would provide a natural model.

"I looked for a system that had a similar flow regime and hence was naturally stable," he said.

Once such a model was found—the East Fork of the San Juan in an adjoining valley—Rosgen set to work, hauling in boulders and parts of old trees to rejuvenate the Blanco's banks and direct its waters toward a more defined channel.

"My goal was to develop a naturally meandering stream that has a close connection to the surrounding riparian environs," Rosgen said. "In the past, methods included using junked cars and concrete to shore up stream banks. That doesn't exactly give the river a natural feel."

One of the main challenges Rosgen faced on the Rio Blanco was filtering out the massive amount of sediment that is carried down from the mountains during spring runoff. If the sediment was not diverted, the streambed would be clogged and water would flow outside of the primary channel. Rosgen and his team constructed a tube to divert cobble, gravel, and sand away from the river channel; water flows through, and sediment is routed to a holding area that can be periodically emptied. The excess gravel—which during my visit rivaled the sand piles along highways during the snow season—is used to supplement the roads and trails around the ranch.

Because of Rosgen's efforts, there are three miles of the Rio Blanco that may be fished by guests of El Rancho Pinoso, which is owned by Robert Lindner Sr., the founder of United Dairy Farms. The price tag for the renovation was about $1 million.

For some, the notion of a river that has felt the shaping hand of man is mildly distasteful, like an overly manicured golf course or a fussily symmetrical garden. On the late September morning that I approached the river with the fly-fishing guide and ranch manager, Damon Scott, I harbored some of these concerns. Would the Rio Blanco be the trout stream equivalent of a miniature golf course—tricked up and obviously artificial?

We crossed the river above our first pool to keep our shadows off the water. Perhaps 20 rainbow trout, illuminated by the sun, finned in the sluice of current that spilled from between the two large boulders that helped form the pool. Scott tied a dry-fly pattern, the Emulator, on my tippet, and several fish proved willing before their interest waned. It was not shooting fish in a barrel, though the trout seemed vulnerable in the slow water.

The next stretch we fished was a different story. This section of stream meandered through a stand of aspens, bending left and right, with several sets of riffles and submerged logs to provide cover: a close-to-perfect trout stream, with the granite face of El Rancho Pinoso's version of Half Dome presiding over the scene.

A trout was delicately sipping small bugs on the surface, just off the edge of one log. Scott tied on an Adams, a great all-purpose dry fly. Because of the current and the log, it was a tricky presentation. After a few tries, I made the right cast. Soon, I was cradling a big-shouldered rainbow, all of 21 inches.

I knew that the fish was not native to the river, and that the river would not exist without Dave Rosgen. But I hardly cared.

Fishing with Lewis & Clark

It had all the makings of a once-in-a-lifetime adventure fishing vacation. The advertising bill might have read:

> *The Louisiana Purchase Territory. Fish uncharted, unexplored rivers for unknown species with former secretary to President Jefferson. Experience authentic aboriginal cultures up close and personal. Eat fresh game each meal. Enjoy occasional dram of whiskey.*

As fate would have it, the Corps of Discovery's route—especially the regions of western Montana traversed in the summer of 1805—comprises what are now considered meccas of western trout fishing. There are outfitters that will gladly guide you and a friend for a week on one of Montana's fabled trout streams—the Beaverhead, the Big Hole, the Bitterroot, for example—for just under $5,000 (lodging, food, and beverages included; fishing licenses, flies, and gratuities extra). That's roughly twice the sum allocated by Congress in 1803 to fund the Corps of Discovery's entire expedition . . . and hooks and fishing line *were* included in the price of the Lewis and Clark trip.

Despite the more pressing matters of exploration, collection, and survival, the journals of Lewis and Clark indicate that some member of the Corps did on occasion find time to fish, and not merely for sustenance:

> *Having nothing further to do, I amused myself in fishing and caught a few small fish; they were of the species of white chub mentioned below the falls, tho' they are small and few in number.*
>
> *Lewis, Wednesday, July 10, 1805*

Journal entries show that Lewis found great satisfaction in fishing—both in his own piscatorial efforts and those of Private Silas Goodrich, who was considered the expedition's most skilled angler. Angling was an escape. The simple focus upon the drift of his bait in the river and the fast and immediate connection with a primitive life force that comes with a hookup must have provided a welcome respite from the heavy responsibilities of leadership. (Many modern business and government leaders find solace in fly fishing for many of the same reasons.) The exploratory nature of angling—never knowing exactly what might take your bait—must have appealed to Lewis's character as well.

While late 18th- and early 19th-century Americans lacked modern conveniences like pizza delivery service and the cash machine that afford us the leisure time we enjoy today, they still found time to pursue recreational activities, including sport fishing. According to fly-fishing historian Paul Schullery, there are records of colonists in New York pursuing sport fishing as early as 1630. Boston established laws to protect common rights to public fishing waters in the 1640s.

By the mid-1700s, there were a number of fishing clubs surfacing in colonial America to provide sport and fellowship for angling aficionados. The greatest concentration of such clubs was in Pennsylvania. In *American Fly Fishing: A History*, Schullery ventures that:

> *Philadelphia, which has given us the most evidence of sport fishing in the Colonies, was by all historical account the primary port of entry for émigrés from Europe until near the end of the 1700s, and that these people and their cultures flourished in the lush valleys and along the now-famous trout waters of south Pennsylvania, and that a high degree of personal freedom in PA permitted great latitude in personal recreation.*

Newspapers of the period show fishing tackle listed for sale, and traveler's journals frequently mention fishing. While a native of Virginia, Lewis spent time in Pennsylvania in the 1790s, and it is quite possible he acquired his interest in angling during his visits. It was from a Philadelphia fishing tackle purveyor named Lawton that Lewis purchased fishing hooks and other assorted gear in 1803; Lawton included a circular advertising his most recent tackle offering with the receipt. That very circular is preserved today.

How Silas Goodrich, a native of Massachusetts, gained his passion for and skill at fishing is open to conjecture. No information has been found that records his date of birth or life prior to his enlistment in the Corps in January of 1804.

Fishermen and women classify themselves into many subcategories. There are people who fly fish, people who fish with lures, and people who fish with bait. There are river anglers, lake anglers, and ocean anglers, anglers who practice catch-and-release (i.e., return their catch mostly unharmed to the water) and those who eat their catch. Against this pantheon of fishing habits, the men of the Corps of Discovery fall squarely in the bait-fishing, catch-eating camp:

> *Goodrich, who is remarkably fond of fishing caught several douzen fish of two different species . . . they bite at meat or grasshoppers.*
>
> *Lewis, Tuesday June 11, 1805*

While perhaps less sporting than fly fishing, bait fishing was certainly a very practical method for the Corps. First, it cut down on packing. No clumsy, fragile rods, no reels, no boxes of meticulously tied flies that had to be kept dry, and certainly none of the silly clothing that often earns fly fishers the derision of their non-fly-casting peers. Silas Goodrich and his companions had the most basic of equipment—fishing line (likely horse hair) and hooks. Bait was plentiful and easy to come by. When grasshoppers or leftover buffalo were not available, Goodrich kept some melt (spleen) of a deer handy, expressly for fishing. Their technique was simple: The angler either spotted a fish or identified a spot likely to hold a fish, baited his fish hook, unlooped some fishing line, and lobbed the baited hook upstream of the intended target, allowing the hook and bait to sink as it floated downstream. When the angler saw a fish swallow the bait or felt a pull on the line, he pulled back, setting the hook in the fish's jaw or gullet. The fish was then played to the boat or shore by pulling the line hand over hand. Visitors to fishing piers along the coast or in lakes with stocked fish will sometimes see the same "hand-lining" technique practiced today. (If someone says that you need a $500 ensemble to catch a trout, you tell them otherwise!)

In addition to being eminently portable and replenishable, bait fishing permitted the Corps of Discovery to fish deep. While fly fishers adore the opportunity to take trout on the surface with gently placed dry flies, fish feed much more frequently below the surface. Goodrich's bait rig enabled him to get down to where the fish were resting more effectively than the flies of the day. Bait also appealed to the fish's olfactory senses. This could not be accomplished with lures and flies.

Until they reached the falls of the Missouri in June of 1805, the Corps of Discovery's angling efforts yielded only species that fish and game regulations generally classify as "trash fish." The chub described in the June 10 entry was actually the first description of a sauger (a member of the perch family). In addition to sauger, the Corps landed numerous catfish, which they prized as food, and goldeye, a member of the mooneye family that resembles a herring. It was near the present-day town of Great Falls, Montana, that trout first appeared on the Corps' fishing radar. On June 13, Lewis reported that

> *Goodrich had caught a half a douzen of very fine trout and a number of both species of the white fish. These trout are from sixteen to twenty three inches in length, precisely resemble our mountain or speckled trout in form and the position of their fins, but the specks on these are of a deep black instead of the red or goald colour of those common in the U.' States. These are furnished long sharp teeth on the pallet and tongue and have generally a small dash of red on each side behind the front ventral fins; the flesh is of a pale yellowish red, or when in good order, or a rose red.*

Goodrich had caught—and Lewis, with his great knack for anatomical detail had described—fine samples of the cutthroat trout, *Salmo clarki*. The "mountain or speckled trout" used for comparison is the brook trout—*Salvelinus fontinalis*. While the cutthroat trout was named for Clark, the men of the Corps of Discovery were not the first whites to encounter it. In his comprehensive natural history study *Trout and Salmon of North America*, fisheries historian and professor emeritus of Fisheries and Conservation at Colorado State University Robert Behnke points out that Francisco de Coronado's expedition came across the Rio Grande cutthroat in the upper Pecos River, south of Santa Fe, New Mexico, in 1541.

Cutthroat were once the preeminent trout species of the western United States. Among angling cognoscenti, they hold a warm spot. They are beautiful, often sprouting intense yellow, orange, and red shades. And they are very willing. A valid scientific study—presumably conducted by some bored postdoctoral students—showed cutthroat the easiest trout to catch by angling methods, followed in difficulty by brook, rainbow, and brown trout. Behnke validates this study, venturing that brown trout are more difficult to catch than cutthroat by at least a factor of ten.

Progress has not been kind to the cutthroat. Today, their distribution is a fraction of what it was in 1805, and two of the subspecies are extinct. Extremely sensitive to changes in water quality, cutthroat have been hurt by stream degradation brought on by logging and livestock grazing. Their great downfall, however, has been brought on by the introduction of nonnative trout species. Anglers casting a fly—or a spot of melt, for that matter—below the great falls of the Missouri will not hook a cutthroat. They have been replaced by brown and rainbow trout.

As the Corps of Discovery pressed further into the Rockies, occasions where Lewis "amused himself in fishing" became less frequent. Trout (and later, salmon) became increasingly significant as a food source, as the new techniques deployed by the Corps might suggest:

> *Late in the evening I made the men form a bush drag, and with it in about two hours they caught 528 very good fish, most of them large trout. Among them I now for the first time saw ten or a douzen of a white species of trout. They are of a silvery coloour except on the back and head, where they are of a bluish cast. The scales are much larger then the speckled trout, but in their form position of their fins teeth mouth they are precisely like them. They are not generally as large but equally well flavored.*
>
> *Lewis, Thursday, August 22, 1805*

When you have 27 hungry men to feed, a hook and line is a less efficient means of procuring protein. Here, in the vicinity of the Salmon River in Idaho, the trout of "silvery coloour" may be the expedition's first encounter with steelhead trout, though mature steelhead are generally much larger than cutthroat trout.

Pushing through the Lolo Pass and on to the Columbia Plateau, the Corps reverted to equally less sporting fishing methods. In his entry for August 26, Clark casually mentions that "one of my men Shot a Sammon in the river about Sunset." Nearly all other fishing references from this point on reference "giging" (*sic*) or spearing. Clark describes the Indian gigging methodology:

> *Their method of taking fish with a gig or bone is with a long pole, about a foot from one End is a Strong String attached to the pole, this String is a little more than a foot long and is tied to the middle of a bone from 4 to 6 inches long, one end Sharp the other with a whole to fasten on the end of the pole with a beard to the large end, the fasten this bone on one end & with the other feel for the fish and turn and Strike them So hard that the bone passes through and Catches on the opposite Side, Slips off the End of the pole and holds the Center of the bone.*
>
> *Clark, August 21, 1805*

From the time they reached the Columbia River on October 16 to their arrival at the Pacific coast a month later, the Corps relied increasingly on salmon for sustenance. Some fish were gigged, but most were purchased or bartered from the many Indian peoples they encountered on the lower river. As the rains of a late Pacific Northwest fall enveloped the Corps, the men seem to have lost their appetite for fishing. Scant mentions of angling appear after they passed the rapids at The Dalles. The men also lost their appetite for salmon. With the exception of Clark, the men showed a preference for the flesh of dogs over the dried flesh of fish.

The Greedy Beady Egg Man

"Eggs, eggs, eggs!"
*Edith Massey (*aka *The Egg Lady),* Pink Flamingos

"I am the Egg Man."
John Lennon

"Eggs are not flies."
Joel La Follette

"Eggs are great for breakfast, but not so good for steelhead." No one actually said that as far as I know, but this is surely the sentiment of the people I fish with. Some of these folks, who would readily identify themselves as dry-liners, greased-liners, purists—*real steelhead fishermen*—would pause to put on anything but a skater, let alone a sinking-tip line or an indicator and an egg, on the end of their lighter-than-advised tippet. They understand that there are people who nymph for steelhead, just as they understand that there's a phenomenon called a "donkey show" in certain border towns and there are men who will water down a good scotch with soda water. The sentiment is: *There are ugly things in this world, but they can be transcended by an adherence to a higher standard, a more regal aesthetic.*

I have always wanted to be a good person, to strive toward a level of moral decency, or what some might term grace. For this reason—and to escape the ridicule of my peers—I swing flies for steelhead. There's no denying that playing a steelhead on a fly rod, *no matter how's it been hooked*, is great fun. But the greatest moment of steelhead fishing—perhaps the greatest moment in *all* fishing—is when that loop leaves your hand, either in agonizingly slow motion, or like you've latched onto a bullet train.

Sometimes I'd meet a guy on the river who would smile and say, "Got five today." Spying the indicator on his rod, I'd smile and say, "Nice." Though, of course, I'd be thinking, "It's easy when you're using gear."

Last fall, I was invited to be part of a movie that was being filmed on Kodiak Island. Using Kodiak Legends Lodge on Larsen Bay as a base, a small camera crew had been capturing iconic images of the island—the Beavers, the long-bearded Russian Orthodox priests, and, of course, the famed bears. There would also be a sporting component of the film, and that's where Conway Bowman (of San Diego mako shark infamy) and Kirk Deeter (of *Angling Trade* and *Field & Stream*, among other illustrious publications) and yours truly entered the picture. We were to fish the Karluk's fall run of steelhead—a run that can sometimes eclipse 10,000 fish, all wild . . . on a river that's just 25 miles long and seldom more than two feet deep. People I knew who had fished the Karluk had mentioned "pocket water"—swinging-fly code for NYMPHING.

I was determined to be pure.

After the Beaver touched down on our first morning, our retinue hiked downstream past a half mile of the knee-deep riffles to a run that formed at a bend in the river. A good *swinging* run. After releasing a left-over silver that took my Starlight Leech on the third cast, my fly swung past a submerged rock. As the line began to straighten, it ripped from my hand. Several jumps later, the trip's first steelhead was at my feet—a 28-inch hen, chrome-bright with nary a hint of red. Two more came to my quavering hands that day. The cameras whirred.

My companions had one fish to hand between them with their eggs.

I would be a celluloid steelhead hero.

When we reached the run the next day, there were four anglers planted firmly in the bucket. We moved downstream, around the next bend, and an endless flat stretched before us. It was here that the egg men went to work. Each time I looked up or down, Kirk and Conway and their Trout Bead rigs were wildly bent over. With a monkish devotion, I kept swinging my leech through the less than 18-inch-deep water. "I'm a good person," a voice within said. "I will achieve grace." Soon the camera crew left my side to focus on the action. I followed after them, trying to explain the subtle virtues of swinging a fly and the greater sport it provided. They smiled and asked Kirk if he could pose with his fish a little to the left.

I wanted to be on camera again. I wanted to hold a fish. I want to be the steelhead god that would be immortalized on the next Fly Fishing Film Tour. Oh vanity!

I followed Kirk to the next little pocket. Sensing my desperation and taking pity, he handed me his rod and said, "Get one out of there." I threw the bobber—*indicator*—above the pocket and made a mend. Five casts later, the indicator was down, and a handsome buck fish was up, thrashing on the surface, a little orange globule bouncing a few inches above the bare hook in its jaw. The camera crew returned, and my metamorphosis toward a new, perhaps less wholesome person had begun.

I had become the greedy beady egg man.

Dylan: The Fly-Fishing Years

Bob Dylan: Folk singer. Protest singer. Betrayer of folk music. Born-again Christian. Orthodox Jew. Victoria's Secret pitchman. Christmas song crooner. Fly fisherman.

Fly fisherman?

There is no photographic evidence of Robert Zimmerman stepping out of a river bearing a brace of trout, boots of Spanish leather glistening; nor are there secondhand tales of a small mumbling man with a bewildering patter and a decent roll-cast, tales shared by grizzled guides after too much bourbon, and only with trusted clients.

No. There are only the songs themselves.

As you will soon see, a close scrutiny of the *music* of Bob Dylan will reveal the *passion* of Bob Dylan—namely fishing. Specifically, *trout* fishing. Especially in the years 1967 to 1976.

"Yea Heavy and a Bottle of Bread"

Recorded in 1967 with the musicians who would come to be known the following year as The Band, "Yea Heavy and a Bottle of Bread" marks Dylan's first unabashed declaration of piscine passion:

It's a one-track town, just brown, and a breeze, too,
Pack up the meat, sweet, we're headin' out
For Wichita in a pile of fruit.
Get the loot, don't be slow, we're gonna catch a trout
(repeated three times)

There's no refuting the narrator's (Dylan's) desire to "catch a trout" (repeated three times!). No wild trout fisheries exist in greater Wichita, nor are there any rivers that boast trout. Thus, it can be deduced that the auteur is comfortable both with stillwater fisheries and stocked fish. The unidentified lake in this case is likely Kansas Department of Transportation East Lake. Some will point out that KDOT East Lake is primarily a baitfishery, calling into question Dylan's commitment to fly angling. However, with "get the loot," the narrator slyly alludes to the high cost of fly tackle—especially in a time before inexpensive graphite blanks from China and Korea.

New Morning

Coming on the heels of the universally panned *Self Portrait* (a record of mostly cover songs), 1970's *New Morning* marks Dylan's return to singing his own compositions. More significantly, it provides the most pointed evidence to date of the Bard of Hibbings' offstage obsession. First, there's "Time Passes Slowly":

Time passes slowly up here in the mountains,
We sit beside bridges and walk beside fountains,
Catch the wild fishes that float through the stream,
Time passes slowly when you're lost in a dream.

Mountains plus wild fishes plus stream unequivocally equals trout. Dylan obviously appreciates the contemplative qualities of angling, an idyll that propels him to a dream state. (NOTE: The "floating fish" above are slightly troubling—are they an allusion to the PCBs that would taint many northeastern streams through the 1960s and '70s?)

"Time Passes Slowly" is followed a few tracks later by "Sign on the Window":

Build me a cabin in Utah,
Marry me a wife, catch rainbow trout,
Have a bunch of kids who call me "Pa,"
That must be what it's all about,
That must be what it's all about.

Here, trout fishing is not merely a pastime. It's interwoven with the very fabric of the narrator's country life, just after his spouse and *ahead of* children. Trout are part of the answer to life's questions, "what it's all about" in the parlance of the day. (It's not hard to imagine Dylan catching it from then-wife Sara for missing the birth of one of those many kids, thanks to a hatch that was simply too prolific to leave.) The location of the "cabin in Utah" has been a point of sometimes violent debate among Dylan scholars. One camp contends that said cabin is on the Provo, close to Salt Lake, the center of Mormonism; they reason that Dylan shows an affinity for the faith (the narrator's desire to "have a bunch of kids"). Others feel the fishery in question is the Green, simply because the fishing is generally better.

"Hurricane"

Dylan's last overt fly-angling allusion comes in "Hurricane," from the 1976 release *Desire*. "Hurricane" marks Dylan's return to protest music as he sings of the plight of Rubin "Hurricane" Carter, a boxer convicted (perhaps wrongfully) of a triple murder:

Rubin could take a man out with just one punch
But he never did like to talk about it all that much.
It's my work, he'd say, and I do it for pay
And when it's over I'd just as soon go on my way
Up to some paradise
Where the trout streams flow and the air is nice . . .

Critics have pointed out that given Carter's inner-city upbringing and penchant for pugilism, a trout stream would not be the first place you'd expect to find him outside the ring. They miss the point. Dylan is projecting his desires onto Carter, imagining himself stepping off the smoke-filled tour bus to make a few casts where "the air is nice."

Who can blame him?

Feed Your Fish Head

Steve lived in a house with fifty other hippies on Haste Street, just west of the Cal–Berkeley campus. It was a hippie house all right, with more bare shingles than paint, and overstuffed couches with sickly green upholstery (was it moss?) overflowing from the house to the weedy front yard. Wind chimes and macramé hangings in the shape of owls were nailed to the porch, and scratchy rock music, mostly the Grateful Dead, floated out of the open windows all day and night, mixing with the night-blooming jasmine, incense, and other smoky smells. A lot of the hippies went naked, as the climate in Berkeley was hospitable to such an undertaking. There were three rules to live by in the house, Steve told me once—no school, no job, and you had to smoke dope. Everybody was on the dole, but with fifty people to pay the rent on a rent-controlled house, there was still plenty left over for jug wine and organic rice and beans, which is all the hippies ever consumed.

They grew their own marijuana in the backyard. Someone had brought Sinsimilla seeds from up north in Humboldt County. One hippie, who had dropped out of the ag program at UC–Davis after dropping too much acid, had rigged up a clever irrigation system with the bathroom fixtures from the house. As personal hygiene was not a priority among the hippies, no one ever seemed to miss the pipes and nozzles that seemed ideally suited for this unique agrarian endeavor. Steve was responsible for pruning the leaves of the plants, a task he performed with a delicate pair of fly-tying scissors.

The small plantation behind the hippie house was no secret on Haste Street, and like-minded neighbors would sometimes stop by and twist off a leaf or two to sample the local crop. "I don't have a problem with it on a philosophical level," Steve said one day in his monotonal rap as he pruned the plants. "Share the women, share the wine, you know? But twisting the leaves off doesn't do anything for the plants. It's bad karma, you know?" Steve was quite satisfied with the plan he came up with to save the plants. "Just Scotch tape a few Js right on the stalk here," he said, pointing to the bottom of the tall plants, which were so strong and healthy that they more resembled small trees than plants. "Then everybody's happy. They get theirs," he said, producing a joint from somewhere in the tie-dyed fishing vest with the Hell's Angels "Frisco" patches, which he always wore. "And the plants keep growing," he added, lighting up and taking a monster toke. "It's like the ultimate recycling, man. HEEHEEHEEHEEHEE!" Steve's laugh, high-pitched and urgent like the cry of a wounded rabbit, still haunts me.

It was the flies Steve tied, not the cannabis, that brought me to the hippie house on Haste Street . . . though I must admit that I would've found several of the female inhabitants desirable as companions had it not been for the low standards of hygiene that prevailed there. I was a junior at Cal at the time, completing a joint major in political science and philosophy. Considering the focus of my studies, I should've been caught up in the various movements unfolding around Berkeley in those days—the Free Speech movement, the antiwar movement, the Free Love movement—but somehow, they didn't register. As far as social awakenings were concerned, I went to bed with the Beatles playing on the *Ed Sullivan Show* and woke up to Watergate.

I attribute a good part of my drowsiness to the discovery of a distant cousin in Del Norte County, just below the Oregon border. This cousin Aloysius—who my parents described as "a distant cousin"—had a rustic cabin not 30 yards from the Smith River, and a pool where the winter-run steelhead stacked up before their last push upriver. Aloysius was a truculent old bastard, more bear than man. Like the hippie house, his cabin lacked plumbing, and Aloysius had his own substantial crop of cannabis growing in a stand of redwoods below the cabin, at the tail of the pool. His horticultural efforts, it turned out, were more mercantile than those of the hippies back in Berkeley. Some years later I would read of his incarceration in the federal penitentiary at Leavenworth, indicted and convicted as the ringleader of Del Norte County's most notorious dope-trafficking ring. I was proud of him, in an odd way, as I didn't think he had the wherewithal.

My proximity to San Francisco—and a flyer describing "Asian Flowers for Companionship or Marriage" that had somehow made the 300-plus-mile trek from Berkeley tucked under the passenger-side wiper blade of my Beetle—had convinced Aloysius that I had an inside track on the Asian mail-order bride market. The concept of a mail-order bride captured his lurid imagination. Aloysius, as mentioned earlier, had a bearlike personage, all hair and blubber, and a demeanor to match. To make matters worse, he carried the most offensive funk about him, a distillation of his modest sanitary habits and the stench of the small animal corpses that were forever strewn about the cabin by his dog, an ungainly mastiff named Pigpen. All these things made him decidedly unpopular with the ladies of Del Norte County. No woman who knew or saw him would have anything to do with him.

The deprivation of female companionship, fueled by prodigious inhalations of his cash crop, further kindled Aloysius' notions of and desire for "an Oriental love slave" (his words, not mine). "Where's my Tokyo Rose?" he'd bellow, hurtling his hulk up the gravel road that led down to his shack like a spawning salmon at the first telltale clatterings of my Bug. "Where's my Shanghai Lil, boy? Where's my Bangkok Bertha? I don't care where she comes from boy, as long as it's turned that slanty way. Argh!" Huffing and puffing in the mist that always seemed to shroud his camp, Aloysius was pitiful, a sad and unrequited Sasquatch.

With his grass and his stench and his roadkill stew (in retrospect I think it was hamburger meat, but he insisted that he had never set foot in a store), Aloysius was not great company. But that didn't matter. I went up there for the Smith, for the long deep pool that stretched seductively from the tip of his rotting porch to the grove of redwoods where Aloysius's crop took root. It was a prime hole that never got fished, because Aloysius had posted the woods on either side of the river with signs reading "Come Down Here and Get Your Ass Shot Off"; he meant it. No one ever came to the hole, so I fished it by myself.

The prime steelhead run—from November to March, depending on the rains—coincided nicely with the academic year. During the season, I would spend the bulk of my time up on the Smith, coming down to Cal just enough to remind my professors that I was alive. I would hole up in the dormitory for April and May to cram enough in my head to pass finals so I could return the following August. This system worked well for me. So well, in fact, that I was invited to stay on after my bachelor's to pursue a PhD in English literature. My thesis explores fishing allusions in Spenser's *The Faerie Queen* as a veiled attack upon the Catholic Church, using Izaak Walton's *The Compleat Angler* as a primary source.

Aloysius, to his credit, had few conditions for my visits. Just a fifth of Wild Turkey to sustain him through the raw nights, and my word that I would stay away from the dope. To sweeten the deal, I would swing over to Chinatown in San Francisco now and then to pick up a few Asian girlie magazines for him before crossing the Golden Gate Bridge and heading north on Route 101. As for the dope, there was plenty of that around Berkeley, had I been interested. The occupants of the hippie house saw to that.

The fact that I resisted the miasma of grass, pills, and powders that engulfed Berkeley in those turbulent times is not testimony to some priggishness or inner fortitude on my part. Quite the contrary, it was a warning sign of my own addiction, namely steelhead (*Oncorhynchus mykiss*). How can I describe the surge of adrenalin that accompanies the take of a three-foot-long steelie, silvery fresh from the Pacific, the rush of its tailwalk upriver, each splash of its tail sending small rainbows swirling skyward? How can I describe the magic Morse code "tap-tap-BOOM" sent fish to man over 30, 60, 80, 150 yards of plastic and monofilament line and eight feet of fiberglass rod, the telegram that reads "BIG FISH . . . STOP . . . HOLD ON FOR YOUR LIFE . . . STOP . . . WHOA!" Why compare it to drugs or sex, or a rise in the stock market, this dancing, electrified vessel of fish flesh? There was nothing, nothing, I preferred to the thrill of hooking and playing a steelhead on the Smith below Aloysius' cabin. I would be there now, had circumstances not rendered fishing implausible.

Though he claimed to have not waded a river since the Eisenhower era, Steve the hippie could tie flies more effective than any I had ever used. I grew up in fly-fishing country, in a small town on the famed

Henry's Fork in Idaho. Most of the town's residents had settled there for the fabulous trout fishing, having walked away from lucrative banking or legal careers on either coast. There was little to do in town but fish or talk about fishing, and as a way of passing time, people would host little fly-tying events. The host was responsible for supplying beer or whiskey and a blown-up photograph of the evening's featured insect. Guests would arrive toting portable vises and baggies full of feathers and fur. The level of minutiae they achieved was amazing, right down to bent antennae and discolorations on the bug's carapace. At the end of the evening, the five best imitations were presented to Leatherjaw, an old rainbow trout that was toted from house to house in a 10-gallon aquarium. He was the final judge.

These fishermen took their craft seriously. When they fished the Henry's, they tucked butterfly nets and portable tying kits into their vests. If a bug showed itself in their midst, the unfortunate creature would be set upon by five or 10 anglers, each lunging with their net. The lucky fishermen who came up with the bug would knot up a replica sensitive to its subtlest nuances in seconds. The craftsmen of Henry's Fork took great pride in their handiwork, the exactitude of which could hoodwink many entomologists, not to mention a good number of trout.

Steve took a radically different approach to fly tying. Instead of replicating the insects that fish prey upon ("matching the hatch," as the phrase goes), he relied on what he called "intuition," which I took to mean getting as stoned as he could stand without passing out, sitting down at his vise, and seeing what happened. His creations were really something, and they got wilder and wilder as the day progressed and he smoked more and more dope.

Some days when I was in town and didn't feel like going to class, I would drop by the hippie house and watch him at work. He'd set up in what had been the downstairs bathroom, the plumbing long removed for the household's agrarian adventures. He had a vise that was fashioned from a roach clip, a cork, and a wine bottle. He used another roach clip for detail work, a small bobbin of thread, and an old syringe. The first time I saw the syringe, my mouth dropped open. Heroin gave me the creeps; a lot of people were killing themselves at the time with an ultrapure variety dubbed Mexican Brown. Steve saw my expression and laughed that laugh of his. "No man," he said. "Never touch the hard stuff. I use it to tie off my flies." He stuck the point of the needle near the eyelet of the hook with his left hand, quickly twisted the thread with his right, and soon handed me another fly, custom prepared for the Smith.

Steve's flies bore no resemblance to any creature that had ever swam, skittered, or flew across a stream. Instead, they took on certain cubist aspects, the shapes of inkblots used by penal system psychiatrists to gage the likely recidivism of violent offenders. In color, they departed sharply from the olives, grays, and browns that ground most patterns in the natural strata. He favored Day-Glo oranges and yellows, hot pinks and electric blues, often combined in a manner that can only be described as psychedelic. (The oranges sometimes used to mimic salmon eggs were pale by his creations.) "It's the color that fish see, man," he would say solemnly before cracking up in peals of wild laughter. There were as close to tie-dyed as a fly could get.

Sometimes Steve would press a fly close up to his thick glasses, a flourish of magenta, neon orange, and hot purple. I was worried he would slip and gore himself with the sharpened hook, but he would just press and stare, sometimes for minutes at a time. When he came out of his trance, he would mumble, "Put my mind in a sling," and place a banged-up 45 of "Mr. Tambourine Man" by Bob Dylan on one of the portable turntables he always kept nearby. He'd sit in the corner, eyes closed, rocking quietly to the music. There would be no more flies that day.

If Steve ever did any fishing, he seldom talked about it, and then only in abstractions. Once he said, "A rainbow fish came walking up the silver stream, lost and lonely exploding three dimensions in a dream." Another time, "He stopped me, first fish of the three, and said, 'We're swimming out to sea!'" His fishing observations didn't reflect my own experiences on the Smith or Henry's Fork, but maybe he'd fished different streams. Deeper waters, so to speak.

Shortly before my sabbatical from the Smith and Berkeley, I stopped by to visit him. By that time, things weren't going too well at the house. The porch was beginning to cave in, and the police had come by and cut down all the cannabis. Neighbors were complaining about the acrid smell that surrounded the house, the smell of 50 long-unwashed bodies. Worst of all, the City of Berkeley was considering some serious revisions of the prevailing rent-control laws. If the ordinances passed and the controls were repealed, rent on the hippie house would double the first year alone. That would mean a lot less money left over for jug wine and organic beans.

There was not much music playing that day when I arrived, and the few strains I heard were dirgeful. The hippies were all out of sorts, just lying around, staring at the ceiling. They hadn't even bothered to take off their clothes. When I found Steve in the basement, I was taken aback. He was stone sober and, perhaps for that reason, abjectly depressed. As I told him about my classes and my last outing on the Smith, he crouched on his haunches in a corner, hovering over a phonograph that played "Ballad of a Thin Man," also by Mr. Dylan. Seeing him like this melted something inside of me. "I'm going up to the Smith this weekend," I stammered. "Do you want to come along?" I had never invited Steve for fear of what might happen with Aloysius and his plants. For that matter, I'd never socialized with him beyond the confines of the hippie house. He smiled a wistful smile and shook his head, fishing a small baggy out of his vest. He passed the baggy to me over the phonograph. Inside were the most fluorescent flies Steve had ever tied for me. They simply lit up the gloomy basement, as if powered by their own tiny battery packs.

My thoughts raced ahead to the smashing results I was certain to see on the Smith. There had been steady rains up north to bring the fish upstream. I knew from experience that the more outlandish Steve's patterns, the more aggressively the fish struck, as if mocking the laws of nature. As I fumbled for the words to express my gratitude, he looked off and spoke, more chanted, in his high-pitched monotone. "It's easy to find food in the rivers or in the sea, but we all need to feed our heads, which isn't always easy in the water. I'm not talking about shrimp and plankton, but the expansive properties of something bigger than all of us. An agent of change, a realization of the outer possibilities. That's what I'm selling. It's all I ask in return."

I said goodbye, and Steve nodded. His arm moved almost imperceptibly to the phonograph, placing the needle back at the beginning of the somber Dylan song before returning to his lap. He was Buddhalike in that basement, in an emaciated, stone sober way.

I've thought a good deal about Steve's statement. Maybe it explained why the steelhead hit his patterns so hard. Maybe his flies were crude fish hallucinogens. Head food, as they say.

Some great philosopher, I can't remember who, said that pity is the most selfish emotion, and that anyone who indulges himself in its sham compassion deserves the worst that befalls them. I went to the Smith that weekend, and as I had predicted, Steve's creations brought the steelhead churning like little silver speedboats. It was my best fishing ever. Before packing up on Monday to return to campus, I found myself at the tail of the pool, by the copse of redwoods that Aloysius had guarded so closely. Had I not been so greedy—had I been satisfied with the 50-plus fat, shiny steelies I had landed and released that weekend—I would have been in my Beetle and gone. But the steelhead were addictive to me and Steve's last batch of flies were casting a remarkable spell. Finding myself so close to the copse and recalling Steve's sorry cannabisless state, I couldn't resist digging up a few plants with my fisherman's utility tool, a gesture at replenishing the lost Haste Street harvest. There were hundreds of plants in that copse. I didn't think Aloysius would ever notice.

Perhaps he didn't. But the DEA agents waiting on the on-ramp of Highway 101 did. Armed with folders of carefully annotated reconnaissance, they were convinced that I was Aloysius' San Francisco connection. Considering my almost weekly trips to Del Norte County, my "untraditional" student lifestyle, and my occasional forays into Chinatown for Aloysius' girlie magazines (the park at Kearny and Washington Streets was a "Grand Central Station for San Francisco dope dealers," as one investigator put it), their deductions were not completely unreasonable. Thanks to the political ambitions of one state's attorney and the general antidrug sentiments that had blown into Northern California on the heels of Altamont, the verdict went against me.

Now I am quietly doing my time in a house of correction in the desert east of Bakersfield. There is a surprisingly well-stocked library here, and I will likely have the opportunity to complete my dissertation before I am paroled. My studies, after all, have little distraction. I suppose I will fish the Smith again someday, though I doubt Aloysius will have finished paying his debt to society in time to entertain me. The fishing, for that matter, may not be as good now. With Aloysius and his menacing signs gone, the pool has doubtlessly been discovered by some intrepid anglers.

There is a small, wiry fellow a few cells down from mine, a murderer. They say he took down three armed men in a barroom brawl, broke their necks with his bare hands. The man, Harry, is pleasant enough, gentle even, which goes to show that you can't ever judge what atrocities a man might be capable of by his exterior. Inside, Harry must be a terror.

Some afternoons we watch television together in the rec room. The Watergate trials are on now, and we take an odd pleasure in them. Whenever two of the defendants, Haldeman and Ehrlichman, are called to the stand, Harry breaks out in mad peals of high-pitched laughter. "Sounds like a vaudeville act," he says, happy tears filling his limpid blue eyes. It *does* sound like a vaudeville act, and that seems to be how Watergate is turning out.

When I hear that laugh, I can't help but wonder if Steve the hippie ever made it out of the basement on Haste Street. Whether he ever waded out again into those streams of the mind that only he could fish.

Among the Hobbit Trout

A Fly-Fishing Pilgrimage to New Zealand's South Island

MAKAROA, NEW ZEALAND—I WAS TROMPING ALONG THE EDGE OF the Wilkin River when guide Paul Wright, treading a few steps ahead of me, held his hand up for me to stop. "I've got a fish here," he called above the steady gurgle of the river. "It's a brownie, I believe. About ten feet out from that rock that's above the water. Can you see it?" The water had a sparkling clarity, an aquamarine hue suggesting the Caribbean more than a mountain stream.

"I can't make it out," I replied. Though the trout was less than 40 feet away—and nearly 24 inches in length—it may as well have been cloaked in an invisible robe to my uneducated eyes as it finned above the rocky bottom in less than two feet of water.

"He looks happy. Give me a cast about ten feet above the rock and 15 feet out from the bank. The current should bring it over him." I made one false cast and dropped the fly above the rock, but a little too close to the bank. "Let it come past and then cast a bit right." When the fly was well beyond the fish's location—at least where Paul *said* the fish was, as I had still not spotted the fish myself—I made a second cast.

"I like that one," he said. Seconds later, a large spotted head popped out of the water and engulfed my beetle fly. I lifted the rod and was fast to a feisty brown trout. My fly rod bent double and line peeled off my reel as the fish tore about the pool, leaping clear of the water twice before coming to Paul's net. It was a thing of beauty—buttery golden skin, dotted with fine black and silver spots. Paul gently removed the fly, revived the fish by holding it by the tail in the current, and the fish beat a hasty retreat, soon blending seamlessly with the river's rocky substrate. We shook hands and continued walking upstream, searching for the next fish.

The South Island of New Zealand has seen an uptick in visitors since the *Lord of the Rings* trilogy—and now, *The Hobbit*—graced the big screen; many fans have been eager to see the sweeping "Middle Earth" scenery featured so prominently in the films. I'm one of 11 people who have not seen Peter Jackson's epics, yet I have still long desired to visit the South Island. Instead of exploring Frodo and Gollum's haunts, I longed to unfurl my fly line on a few of its countless trout streams. Like so many Kiwi inhabitants, both rainbow and brown trout were imported to the island nation in the 1800s, from California and Great Britain, respectively. With no natural predators, the fish have thrived. The average South Island trout stream does not contain enough forage to sustain large numbers of fish, but the trout that are present are quite large, averaging three to six pounds, with fish in the eight- to ten-pound range encountered every year. It's the combination of big fish, spectacular scenery, and crystalline streams that allow anglers to stalk their prey that has made New Zealand—and the South Island, in particular—a bucket-list destination for diehard trout anglers.

Chris Daughters, guide, fly shop proprietor, and now owner of Cedar Lodge in Makaroa, was first drawn to the South Island more than 20 years ago. "I'd just finished college, and had heard it was a great place to go for a fishing vacation on the cheap," he recalled. "Some guys from the fly shop [where Daughters was then an employee] and I saved our pennies, and spent three months that winter bumming around, fishing. I was captivated with the landscape, the friendly people, and the quality of the fishing. Some years later, my wife, Shauna, took me to Cedar Lodge to celebrate my 40th birthday, and I was taken with the spot. Its location on the border of Mount Aspiring National Park provides fantastic access to a great diversity of water—big braided rivers flowing into the region's vast lakes, intimate streams in steep valleys, and wild, seldom-visited rivers on the west side of the Southern Alps that drain into the Tasman Sea."

A few years later when Cedar Lodge came up for sale, Daughters purchased the property. Now, he and his family (including daughter Patsy and son Cash) split their time between Makaroa and Eugene, Oregon. Chris coordinates fishing activities and sometimes guides; Shauna oversees day-to-day lodge operations and homeschools the kids; Patsy (age 10) sometimes ties flies for clients.

Cedar Lodge holds a venerable place on the roster of New Zealand fishing lodges. Established in 1979, its founder, Dick Fraser, helped pioneer heli-fishing on the South Island. A helipad rests at the south end of the property, separated from the lodge itself by a five-hole "rural" golf course (where a few passes of the lawnmower create fairways and greens) that doubles as a sheep paddock in the off-season. Cedar Lodge is intimate; four comfortably appointed rooms, each with a bathroom and deck overlooking the mountains, can accommodate a maximum of eight guests. Meals are taken in the lounge area in the center of the structure or, on clear evenings, at an outside dining area. A host of non-fishing activities are available, including wine tasting in the Central Otago region (just over the mountains to the east); spa days in the resort town of Wanaka; four-wheel-drive tours of local farms where cattle, sheep, and red stag are raised; and eco-tours ranging from heli-hiking to jet boat trips. Even bungee jumping excursions can be arranged—the the pastime's first commercial operation was established a few hours south in Queenstown.

But the great majority of visitors come to Cedar Lodge to fish.

A day at Cedar Lodge begins with a hearty breakfast; a favorite during my stay was a breakfast sandwich featuring locally farmed eggs, bacon, avocado, and tomato chutney on a freshly baked croissant. (Chef Steve Weiler makes a special effort to highlight local ingredients in his cuisine.) While guests enjoy a second cup of coffee, Daughters and his guides share the day's itinerary. With miles of fishable water on a dozen rivers to choose from, the day's destination is determined by weather conditions and how recently the rivers have been fished. Anglers then don their fishing togs—polypropylene long underwear and nylon shorts with wading boots are favored over traditional waders as the air is warm, the rivers not too cold, and a fair bit of hiking is involved. Then each pair of anglers heads across the golf course to the helipad to embark on the day's adventure.

The helicopter—an R44 Raven II—is a key ingredient in the Cedar Lodge angling experience, permitting rapid access to stretches of river that might otherwise take days to reach by foot . . . if they could be reached at all! On my first day out, pilot/guide Dion Matheson provided the basic rules for safe heli-travel: hold your hat as you're approaching the copter, let your guide load your gear in the storage department, use the handle (not the door) to pull yourself in, attach your seatbelt, pop on your headphones . . . and enjoy the views. Seconds after strapping in, we were off, soaring above the Makaroa River that borders the lodge property before banking right into the wide valley formed by the Wilkin. There's a saying among Kiwi helicopter pilots—"the wind begins in Makaroa"—and indeed, it was howling that morning. But Matheson hugged a hillside festooned in beech trees to assure safe passage. Shifting clouds revealed the peaks of snowcapped mountains beyond the green hills. After five minutes, we set down. The scenery was every bit as dramatic as I've witnessed in the trout havens of Montana and Alaska, with the added bonus that there were no bears or other critters in the woods with the capacity to kill me! There were no other anglers for miles.

It must be said that fishing on the clear rivers of the South Island is challenging. As alluded above, the trout on these systems are few and often far between. That means a fair bit of streamside hiking (with occasional bushwhacking) as you move upstream to find fish. I averaged at least two or three miles each day on the river, sometimes scrambling 50 yards behind guide Paul Wright, who positively bounded over boulders and brush along the banks. Once you do locate a fish—or once your guide locates a fish—it takes a careful cast to entice the fish to bite. "There are three P's for hooking trout on these rivers," Wright said, when I asked him the secret to success. "Presentation, presentation, and presentation!" First, the angler must drop the fly gently above the fish so the current can carry it down. If you slap the line down on the water, the trout will be startled and put off. The angler must also control the downstream path of the fly—the "drift," in angling parlance—so the fly appears as if it's floating naturally in the current. If you do all these things right and the fish is willing, you must be careful not to set the hook too quickly, lest you pull the fly out of the trout's mouth. "If you wait the amount of time it takes to say 'God Save the Queen,'" Daughters said, "you're about right."

This style of fishing requires tremendous focus. But Wright pointed out the importance of looking up from time to time. "If you're missing the scenery, you're only getting half the experience," he said.

On my last day, Daughters and I fished an unnamed river west of the crest of the Southern Alps. As the helicopter darted through a small hole in the low-lying clouds, we were greeted by a riot of green, the dense beech forests punctuated with lighter-colored cabbage tree palms. At one point, Daughters spotted a large brown trout in a pool below a huge boulder. Thick brush enveloped the shoreline. "The only way you can get to the fish is to crawl down through the brush to that rock outcropping and make a sidearm cast. I call it hobbit fishing." I gently dropped down to the rock in question and made a cast without tangling the fly in the brush behind me. The current slid the fly a bit to the right of the fish. "Try again, more right," Daughters said. The second cast was dead on. The fly drifted right over the fish, but it was unimpressed and swam slowly across the river, in plain view but out of range.

If it was easy, catching a hobbit trout wouldn't mean as much.

But the defeats are as compelling as the victories when recounted over drinks back at the lodge. After swapping a few fish tales at happy hour (with the guides present to prevent said tales from becoming too tall), there was time for a few holes of golf—and a few more indignities in my case—before chef Steve served up an entrée of pan-fried, panko-crusted red stag. Though usually squeamish around venison, I found this dish delicately prepared and well paired with a local, award-winning Akarua Pinot Noir. The murmur of the Makaroa was barely audible in the background as the setting sun glinted off the peaks of the Southern Alps to the west. Peter Jackson couldn't have scripted a better ending to a South Island day.

Rainbows All

One Angler's Steelhead Metamorphoses

If you live in Portland, Oregon, and like to fly fish, odds are good that you consider the Deschutes your home river . . . even though the Deschutes is at least 100 miles away. There are other streams closer to town in the Cascades or Coast Range that have populations of scrappy native cutts, and several Willamette Valley rivers that host seasonal steelhead runs. But these watersheds don't have the drawing power of the big D.

One part of the draw—especially come late summer—is that the Deschutes offers both high-quality trout fishing *and* a world-class steelhead fishery. And that all this angling abundance unfolds in an inhospitably arid rimrock canyon, where the presence of water—let alone ocean-going rainbow trout—seems a small miracle.

Like so many fly anglers, my entrée to the pastime came through trout fishing. My home river during high school was the Saugatuck—more specifically, a mile or so stretch of the Saugatuck that flowed behind a Westport, Connecticut, corporate park. (Little did I know that at the same time, just a few miles away, Martha Stewart was launching her catering career.) I had little idea what I was doing, and when my wildly swung Royal Coachman streamer (a pattern I haven't seen since) was engulfed by a sickly brown trout fresh from the hatchery, my less than idyllic surroundings hardly mattered.

The Deschutes and its beautiful, native redband strain of rainbow trout (*Oncorhynchus mykiss gairdneri*) were certainly a step up from the Saugatuck and its planters. My first spring and summer in Portland (just before children), I'd make the 2-plus-hour run to the river around

Maupin at the drop of a hat. Salmonflies still coming off? I can make it. Morning PMDs? No one from the home office will miss me too much. Evening caddis? I'll make the sandwiches and buy the beer. Though by this time I had a better grasp of the concept of the dead drift, catching fish was far from a guarantee. But the grandeur of the Deschutes' canyon country (including the general absence of corporate parks) and the pulling power of the occasional fish that was gulled by an elk-hair caddis or pheasant tail more than compensated for my modest levels of success.

Later that fateful summer, steelhead began returning to the Deschutes in fishable numbers . . . and all the enthusiasm and respect I'd garnered for the river's redsides was all but thrown out the window.

Much has been written about the appeals of steelhead as a game fish. Their inscrutability. The terrific ferocity of their take. Their propensity for long, leaping runs. Their *occasional* proclivity for skated flies and the many ways they'll take them (sip, slam, bathtub swirl, etc.). And of course, the many variations of their beautiful form, from chrome-bright, fresh-from-the-sea fish with only the slightest hint of magenta along their gill plates to darker specimens that closely resemble an inflated version of resident rainbows, with an equally pronounced red band along their flanks. No surprise, given that from a taxonomic perspective both rainbow trout and steelhead are classified as *Oncorhynchus mykiss*, the same species that over time have adopted different lifestyles. (On that note: conventional wisdom has posited that the "steelhead lifestyle" was adopted by rainbow trout that lived in rivers that had access to the Pacific and eventually made their way seaward. Some recent research has suggested the opposite; that all rainbows were once steelhead, but for some, the path to the ocean became blocked and different landlocked habits evolved.)

I had harbored a lingering curiosity about steelhead for many years before I began haunting the Deschutes in 1999; indeed, I drove from Connecticut to British Columbia in 1989 in hopes of landing one of these silver ghosts. A friend and I made our way north to the fabled waters of the Kispiox, where we had the river completely to ourselves . . . this largely a result of it being July, and the fact that any steelhead returning to the Kispiox were still in the vicinity of the Queen Charlotte Islands. (Apparently, neither of us could read or use a telephone at the time.) When this curiosity metamorphosed into an actual fish—taken on a skater, no less—I was changed.

In May or June, perhaps even early July, I will make my way to the Deschutes to breathe in the dry sage air and roll the dice with the salmonfly or PMD hatches that *might* transpire. But once the Fish Passage Center at Bonneville shows 1,000 steelhead a day passing over the dam, the trout gear is pretty much forgotten, supplanted by a 7-weight spey rod.

The tug *is* the drug.

Over many long hours of hiking the Burlington Northern Sante Fe tracks on the west side of the river in search of a promising run, of stepping, casting, and swinging (and repeating . . . 500 times), of scanning the canyons for bighorn sheep (when I should be paying attention to my swing), I've had ample opportunity to consider my transition from trout angler to steelheader. I believe it follows from the following frailties of character:

Laziness: Much is made about the difficulty of steelhead fishing. It would be more accurate to characterize the complexity of *catching* a steelhead. Steelhead fishing itself is largely a brainless activity, especially once you have a sense of the spey cast and a familiarity with the kind of water where the fish might hold. Little concern need be given to the type of bug you affix to your leader, the stage of the insect's life cycle, its nuances of color or form. Many steelheaders (me included) place little significance on fly selection, beyond lighter color during low light and darker color during high light. Likewise, anglers don't need to dedicate much concern to perfecting their dead drift. Just cast and let it swing. The benefit of minimal thinking even extends to the moment of truth when a fish grabs your fly. The surest way to part company with a steelhead taking a swung fly is to lift the rod in an attempt to set the hook; the best steelheaders know that the best way to hook up is to do nothing. Just let 'em go . . . or if you're the kind of steelheader who holds a loop of line, just let the loop go. Talk about the Zen of fly fishing!

A Perverse Appreciation of Chance: Over the years, I've tried to believe that my preference for steelheading signified something slightly noble: an inclination to defer small pleasures for the thrill of the big grab; a willingness to eschew the more modest accomplishments of a 13-inch trout for the outsized achievement of a 33-inch chrome-bright buck, a few sea lice still clinging to its flank. It's comforting to a fragile ego to think so, but I believe the truth is that I appreciate steelheading for the same reasons I enjoy golf, music, and my work as a freelancer . . . the utter randomness of modest success. The role of chance. To take the golf example: my scores can range anywhere from 88 to 105. Some of that, admittedly, depends on the difficulty of the course, though a lot depends on which Santella shows up on any given day. I'm not a very good golfer, but some days I'll go out and play pretty well . . . and there's always that potential. It's that potential for good results that drags me out to the course again and again.

The word "hope" here might be substituted for "potential."

Trout fishing—at least when it's done in an earnest manner—is a focused, even analytic endeavor. Unless you're on a remote cutty creek in the Rockies or just about anywhere in Alaska, to find success—if we're equating success with catching—you need to pay attention, adjust tactics . . . *think*. Those who do will likely find fish; those who don't are destined to enjoy a pleasant day outside. In other words, some if not much of the responsibility for the outing's outcome rests with the angler.

In my steelhead experience, anglers of modest ability/experience are largely absolved of accountability in the quest to bring a steelhead to hand. Yes, you have to be able to cast; yes, you have to understand where the fish like to rest. But beyond that, you have to let go. There may not be any fish in the run you've hiked three miles to reach . . . or they may have had three other anglers swing past them. You cast, step, and hope. I can't tell you how many times my cronies and I have fished near the mouth of the Deschutes, with perfect conditions, access to the best water, and a sense that we were fishing well . . . with nothing to show. On other occasions, we've flipped the fly in front of us to pull line off the reel in preparation for fishing and have been *riiiiippppped* (in the parlance of the younger steelhead devotees) . . . or have left the fly to dangle at the end of its swing to take a swig of water or scratch our nose, only to find ourselves fast to a fish as we prepare to cast.

It's a funny game that way. Not for those who crave order and a clear line of causation. Not for those governed by logic.

But well-suited for me.

The Rainbows of Crater Lake

"Not a bad view," guide Ethan Barrow called down to me from one of the basalt bluffs on Wizard Island. I looked up from the crystalline, Caribbean-like waters of Crater Lake to take in the almost 1,000-foot walls of the caldera. "Fish coming from the left, 10 o'clock!" Ethan cried. Trying to refocus from the cliffs on high to the clear water below, I experienced a brief bout of vertigo, nearly toppling into the 50-degree water from the rock I was perched upon. After steadying myself, I asked Ethan if the fish were still there. "He went down," Ethan called back. "But a nice one is cruising in from the right." I launched my best steeple cast in the direction of the shadow that was clearly morphing into a large trout.

Crater Lake National Park sits in the Cascade Mountains of southern Oregon, roughly an hour north of the city of Klamath Falls. The lake itself rests at the bottom of a six-mile-wide, 8,000-foot-tall caldera. Shimmering in hues of incredible blue at the bottom of a crater that varies from 500 to nearly 2,000 feet in height, the lake is wonder-of-the-world-inspiring; your first glimpse may leave you speechless. There are two stories of how Crater Lake came to be. The Klamath People, one of the Native American tribes that call the region home, tell a legend of two Chiefs, Llao of the Below World and Skell of the Above World. They became pitted in a battle that ended in the destruction of Llao's home, 12,000-plus-foot-tall Mt. Mazama. The mountain's destruction led to the creation of Crater Lake. Geologists believe that an ancient volcano (posthumously named Mount Mazama) erupted. The basin or caldera was formed after the top 5,000 feet of the volcano collapsed. Subsequent lava flows sealed the bottom, allowing the caldera to fill with approximately 4.6 trillion gallons of water from rainfall and snow melt, creating the ninth-deepest lake in the world.

Crater Lake sees an average of 44 feet of snow a year; it's the snow melt that gives the lake its incredibly vibrant shades of blue. The Klamath Indians revered the lake and the surrounding area, shielding it from non-Native explorers until 1853, when three gold prospectors stumbled upon the lake. (Crater Lake is known as *Giiwas* in the Klamath language, which means "Spiritual Place.") But gold was more on the minds of settlers at the time and the discovery was soon forgotten. Captain Clarence Dutton, commander of a U.S. Geological Survey party, was the next known Euro-American to visit Crater Lake. From the stern of his survey boat the *Cleetwood*, Dutton sounded the depths with lead pipe and piano wire. His recording of 1,996 feet was amazingly close to sonar readings made in 1959 that established the lake's deepest point at 1,932 feet.

I've lived in Oregon for 17 years, and though I've visited Crater Lake in the past, I had always thought the lake was sterile. Thus I was taken aback when Ethan enthused about the fishery. "There are a lot of 20-inch fish in Crater Lake, and the fishing pressure is very light," he said. "I tell people that fishing there is about the sights—the sight of the lake from above and the caldera from the lake surface, and the sight-fishing for big rainbows."

The rainbow trout of Crater Lake are not native to the system. The first fish are believed to have been introduced from the Rogue River by one William Steel. "Steel is the man most responsible for having Crater Lake established as a national park," said Mark Buktenica, an Aquatic Ecologist with the National Park Service. "He spent 20 years of his life—and a good deal of his own money—promoting the idea, including a number of trips back to Washington, D.C. Crater Lake was fishless when Steel first fell in love with the place. There are no surface outlets leaving the caldera, thus there's no way for fish to find a way in. To the best of our knowledge, Steel went to the Rogue sometime in 1888 with a bucket and collected 600 fry, then carried them up (and then down) to the lake on horseback, stopping to collect fresh water from creeks along the way to sustain the fry. The assumption is that Steel thought the lake would be more attractive for the gentleman traveler of the time—who had the means to travel across country and stay in a nice lodge—if fishing was available." Between that time and 1941, nearly two million trout and salmon were stocked on an irregular basis. Though no fish have been stocked since, the rainbows have been able to successfully shore spawn. Introduced kokanee also spawn successfully.

The biggest rainbow Buktenica and his staff have encountered was 24-inches.

A fishing day at Crater Lake is just as much a hiking day. First, you must reach the lake. The Cleetwood Cove Trail down drops 700 feet over 1.1 miles, hard on the knees if not the lungs . . . though you are at 6,000 feet. While there is limited fishing access at the bottom of the trail, serious anglers will take one of the tour boats to Wizard Island. The September day I hiked down the trail with Ethan and two other guests, Ralph Brooks and Sara Mckenzie from Beaverton's River City Fly Shop, the sun shone bright, accentuating the lake's sparkling waters. The 30-minute ride to the island allowed for many perspectives of the caldera. Upon arrival, our group—and three other anglers—began scrambling in a northerly direction toward several coves that had proven fertile grounds on Ethan's past expeditions. (A maximum of six anglers are allowed on Wizard Island each day.) Wizard Island is itself a remnant volcano, and the going on the sharp, uneven rocks is not easy. (Put another way: this is *not* sandal country.)

When we reached the cove, each angler was positioned on a point, allowing a bit of room for a backcast . . . though the aforementioned steeple cast came in handy, as the shoreline is steep. From the rocks above, Ethan had the Crater Lake equivalent of the poling platform vantage, and could call out approaching fish that came in from the depths seeking crayfish in the relative shallows. Casting one of Ethan's crayfish patterns, Sara was the first to draw action. A fish in the 20-inch range boiled on her fly four times, nearly marooning itself on the rock she was balanced upon. "Gotta set a little slower," Ethan advised. Fifty yards down the cove, Ralph soon hooked and landed a 22-inch specimen, which was promptly dispatched. (Catch-and-take fishing is encouraged at Crater Lake, as the fish are technically invasive species, though there are no plans to remove them by any means other than angling.) I had a number of follows on my crayfish and a few premature sets. The bright sun, while enhancing our visibility, was likely making the fish a bit more wary. Though my morning ended fishless, there were enough sightings and shots to feel like I was in the game.

That afternoon, as our group moved to a new cove, fish began dimpling the surface for as far as I could see. Many seemed just beyond our best double hauls; and since waders or any personal craft are forbidden in Crater Lake, they stayed that way. Those that were in reach were mostly indifferent to our offerings. As best as we could tell, the fish were taking carpenter ants or termites in the film. Even Sara and Ralph, both excellent tiers, were unable to crack the code. After a half hour of frustration, I was happy to kick back and enjoy the vistas. By 2:30, we were hoofing it back to the boat landing, as the last boat departs Wizard Island at 3:30.

The 700 vertical feet back to the rim had my heart rate up—somewhat embarrassingly so. But not too many of the French septuagenarians (from a bus tour) who'd made the trek down to the lake overtook me, and the extra effort made the Mirror Pond Ales at the historic Crater Lake Lodge that much more refreshing. Sitting on the lodge patio high above the lake, I was unable to resist buttonholing passersby: "See that island? I was down there fishing today. And the trout are huge!"

It Was *Epic, Dude*!

I CAN'T RECALL EXACTLY WHEN THE LANGUAGE OF FLY FISHING WAS hijacked by surfers. But there's little question that it's happened. Encounter any group of 18- to 49-year-olds—male or female—at a river takeout, and ask them how the fishing was. If their fishing was even modestly productive, the response will inevitably be, "It was *EPIC, DUDE*!" Or, in a variation that may stem from geographic nuances (or the availability of medical marijuana), "*DUDE*, it was *EPIC*!"

The *"EPIC"* descriptor is not limited to the broader fishing experience. Hatches can be *EPIC.* Catching a 7-inch brook trout on a tenkara rod can be *EPIC.* Finding a cold beer hidden under the apples in the cooler when you thought there were none can be *EPIC.* The drive down a rutted river access road can be *EPIC* (though *GNARLEY* is an acceptable substitution). A snarl in one's tippet can be *EPIC.*

And, as it probably goes without saying, any male angler, fly shop employee, guide, bartender, gas station attendant, or fish-and-game official under the age of 80 can be a *DUDE.*

To better understand these exciting new idioms, it makes sense to look at their provenance. According to Douglas Harper's *Online Etymology Dictionary*, the adjective "epic" dates to the 1580s, "pertaining to or constituting a lengthy heroic poem," via Middle French *épique* or directly from Latin *epicus*, from Greek *epikos*, from *epos*: "a word; a tale, story; promise, prophecy, proverb; poetry in heroic verse." As early as 1706, it was referenced as a noun, referencing an epic poem: "A long narrative told on a grand scale of time and place, featuring a larger-than-life protagonist and heroic actions." So epic has its roots in a literary tradition and speaks to great acts and gestures of heroism. It's the stuff of *The Illiad* and *The Odyssey*, of overcoming centaurs, sirens, and Cyclops with simple weapons. It is, perhaps, the stuff of landing a three-figure tarpon on an eight-pound test tippet; it is arguably not the stuff of palm-sized brookies landed on tenkara rods or any other tackle, for that matter . . . unless those fish were caught after a three-week hike through the wilds of Labrador with no food, water, or clothing.

"Dude" has an equally interesting derivation. Contrary to popular opinion, the term *does* have roots earlier than 1998, the year the Coen brothers film *The Big Lebowski* was released. In the journal *Comments on Etymology*, Barry Popik and Gerald Cohen have provided the most definitive explanation of "dude." It appears that the word is derived from "doodle," as in "Yankee Doodle Dandy"—the fellow who "stuck a feather in his cap and called it macaroni." In 18th-century England, "macaroni" was a slang term for a dandy, coined for young Brits who traveled to the Continent and came back wearing pretentious clothes and possessing an appetite for a certain carbohydrate-rich dish of Italian origins. (Colonists, lacking access to fine haberdashery and pasta, could only muster a feather in an attempt to imitate the *macaronis*.) In New York, in the early 1880s, the short-form "dood" was applied to foppish young men. It was sometimes spelled "dude." "Dude" (or "dood"), then, would seem to be a noun more at home in urban environments—say the Paris or London of Oscar Wilde—rather than the trout Meccas of Maupin or Island Park. Most would not describe the waders, wading jackets, or vests favored by most riverine anglers as overly dandyish—though exception might be made for some of the new slings on the market, which do have a metrosexual quality about them. Given this, "dude" may not be apropos for fly anglers, unless they are walking along an English chalk stream, clad in tweeds and ascots.

I'll be the first to admit that I may be a crank. At 52, I've timed out on conventional dude usage (*dudage*?), though I am still sometimes referenced as such, despite being a dull and even slovenly dresser. There are few if any aspects of my day-to-day behavior—on the river or off—that faintly approach the grand or heroic . . . though as an English major, I have in the past read (if not necessarily enjoyed) my share of *epic* poems.

Perhaps it's that English major background that makes me cringe even before that fateful phrase is uttered. Conservatively speaking, there are over 170,000 words in the English language. Of these, the average native English speaker actively uses some 20,000. With such an arsenal at the angler's disposal, it would seem possible that we could aspire for not only a richer fishing language, but a more accurate one. Imagine approaching a take-out on the Upper Delaware. You ask the sturdy young men bounding out of a drift boat about their day. "The fishing was inconsistent in the upper reaches," one replies, "but as the *Ephemeralla lata* emerged, we found a number of feeding fish, some of which were tricked by our imitations." "The scent of the air was exhilarating," his companion, adds, "redolent with summer, yet hinting at the autumn to come."

Now, that would be *KICK-ASS*.

The Pledge

I WAS INTERVIEWING NOTED FLY-TIER/TRAVEL EXPERT KEN MORRISH A few months back about the evolution of the Morrish Mouse. Somewhere in the course of our conversation, he ventured that for a long time he didn't think you could catch rainbows on a mouse fly, and hence never used them. This, of course, beget a self-fulfilling prophecy. "If you don't fish mouse flies, you're definitely not going to catch fish on mouse flies," he added. "When I started using mouse patterns, I began catching fish on them . . . at least sometimes."

I began applying this logic to steelhead and the use of skating flies. It's a tremendous thrill to watch a steelhead grab—or try to grab—a skater . . . maybe one of the sport's greatest thrills. Sometimes it's a toilet bowl take, where the fly is engulfed in a vacuum three feet across as it's sucked down. Sometimes it's a bump on the nose on three straight swings, followed by nothing. Or the gentlest mayfly sip—followed by a pause—followed by the scream of angler and reel that announces to the world "Fish on!" . . . which is all the more satisfying if you've logged six or seven hundred toward the fish of a thousand casts. My very first steelhead came to hand on a skater on the North Umpqua in 1999, and I've found a few Deschutes fish on top over the years, tying on the odd Moose Turd after landing a fish or two on a swung Freight Train, my most trusted Deschutes pattern.

But I hardly ever fish skating flies for steelhead.

And that means that I hardly ever catch steelhead on skating flies.

For years, some of my angling cronies have made the case for fishing skating flies for summer steelhead *all the time*. Swung wet flies on a floating line and leader are seldom more than six inches under the surface, they argue. If a fish can see these, surely they can see the skater, which creates even more attention with its gurgling, bubbling whipping-across-the-water antics. The fish are aggressive and will move to a fly.

An added bonus for the angler—when you're skating, you can see *exactly* what kind of a swing you're getting, and mend accordingly. The feedback is instantaneous.

Though I lacked confidence in the skating fly, I was ready to commit. But recognizing the frailty of the human condition—namely, my great potential for backsliding—I realized the need to somehow cement my commitment. And no cement would be as strong as a gentleman's agreement: a pledge. And I needed to look no further than over my back fence to find a co-conspirator. My neighbor Geoff Roach is a committed steelhead angler, had shown interest in skating flies, and had even been fooling around with a skating pattern of his own, a hybrid of the Ska-Opper (popularized on the North Umpqua) and the Freight Train, which we dubbed the Fropper. The pledge was simple: Geoff and I would fish only skating flies—specifically, the Fropper—until one of us took a steelhead on top.

This was May. We did not sign our names in blood, though I do recall beer being involved.

In early July, I made my first foray to the mouth of the Deschutes with another angling buddy, Mike Marcus. We accepted that only small numbers of fish would be present, but had heard reports of a few steelhead being taken . . . and the early-run fish, generally natives, were known for being particularly inclined toward skaters. I removed the slow-sinking leader from my little 7-weight spey outfit and attached a long floating leader and a Fropper. Mike rigged his with a fast-sinking leader and a small, lightly weighted leech. Stepping into one of my favorite runs, I began working out line. I was happy with the Fropper's performance; it had minimal wind resistance and waked nicely on the surface, especially on the tailout . . . the kind of faster, slick water that's custom-made for skaters. But soon I had concerns: on choppy water in the run where I'd hooked a number of fish in the past, the Fropper didn't skate or do much of anything at all; I was concerned whether fish could pick it up through the chop. Ditto, the slower water below riffles, where so often, my Freight Train had dragged almost to a halt before being whacked. As the sun dipped behind the canyon walls to the west, I found it increasingly difficult to follow the fly. I'd track a spot in the water two-thirds of the way through the swing, only to see the bug pop up 20 feet beyond.

Then came the moment of truth. I worked through a slick above some rocks at a spot we call the Junction Hole, one of my cabal's most reliable spots. Nothing. Mike came behind me with his sub-surface setup. Near the end of the third or fourth swing, the loop of line was yanked from his hand, though he didn't quite hook up. There was little doubt it was a steelhead.

There was more good water below. For a moment, I wavered. There were fish present. The bit of empirical evidence we had suggested they were lower in the water column. Logic would dictate that I place my fly accordingly. But I was not operating under the simple dictates of logic. I was adhering to *the pledge*.

Any temptation the situation presented was erased by the fact that I'd removed my sinking poly leader and my fly box filled with Freight Trains from my wader pocket. My arsenal at that moment was a spool of tippet and two more Froppers tucked into my shirt pocket.

I moved nothing to the Fropper that evening as the late lingering July light bled from the sky into the distant Pacific. To make matters worse, I fell in twice, water gushing into my Simms like so many tears of laughter from the steelhead gods.

Before I'd even reached the parking area, I found myself dissecting the pledge for loopholes:

- Would I be allowed to take off the Fropper if I (or someone else) raised a fish but didn't hook it and I wanted to make a second pass through?
- Did the pledge apply to other rivers or only the Deschutes?
- Did the pledge apply to odd days of the month?

This before Geoff had even wet a line.

A few weeks later, Geoff made his first his trip to the mouth. I was unable to join him and waited eagerly for a report. Over the course of a weekend-long outing, he hiked nearly 30 miles up and down the river, vigorously skating his Fropper across Rattlesnake, Hot Rocks, Steelie Flats, and other fabled runs. Or so I thought.

"I fished the Fropper on Friday night and Saturday morning," he confided. "But it got to the middle of the day and the sun was on the water, and I put on a Freight Train. And I just left it on." The good news was, on Sunday morning he'd hooked and landed a small native fish in Hot Rocks. The pledge had been broken, and not by me. I could claim the moral high ground.

And more importantly, I could return to my beloved Freight Train and fish with confidence. And save the Fropper for those occasions when I already had a fish or two to hand.

No Good Deed Goes Unpunished

WHILE I LOVE TO WRITE FOR FINE FLY-FISHING PUBLICATIONS LIKE *Flyfish Journal* and *Fly Rod & Reel*, it's especially exciting to land a fly-fishing piece in the mainstream media. In outlets like *The Washington Post* or the *New York Times*, it's certainly not for the money. It's about stroking my ego. Instead of thousands or tens of thousands of eyes, it's hundreds of thousands if not millions of *pairs* of eyes hanging on each twist and turn of my turgid prose. Appearing in those hallowed pages always gives me a sense of having arrived; I'm less than half an inch (in total page width) from Bob Woodward, Paul Klugman, and other establishment scribblers. Such placements also bring a few e-mails from long lost friends . . . and occasionally the fund-raising arms of my various alma maters, who mistakenly equate such publications with wealth.

Nonetheless, it was with no small excitement that I learned a piece I'd submitted to *The Washington Post* about a fishing experience at Cedar Lodge on the South Island of New Zealand was going to run in the Sunday, January 11 edition. I visited the *Post* website on Saturday night and sure enough, there it was: "Fly Fishing in New Zealand: Emphasis on the 'Fly.'" (Cedar is a fly-out lodge.) No hero shot of Santella with one of his six-pound browns, but still looking good. Even my cliché (but mildly clever) *Lord of the Rings* allusion had survived the cut. When I picked up the hard copy edition on Sunday morning, I was surprised to see that the story occupied an entire page of the *Post*'s Travel section. I whimsically imagined that I might get a call from the New Zealand Minister of Tourism, thanking me for a story that—were it a paid ad placement—might have cost nearly $100,000, and would reach over one million readers . . . and that's before the 20-odd-million monthly web visitors.

Sure enough, that evening I did receive an e-mail from someone at New Zealand Fish & Game. It began:

Congratulations on your story on NZ fly fishing which was published in the Washington Post. I'm sure that will generate a bit of interest in New Zealand angling.

A good start, if somewhat understated. The next paragraph took a decidedly less positive tone:

Secondly, and more importantly, I need for you to contact me rather quickly about your recent fishing trip to the Wilkin River in New Zealand. I have checked our database and cannot find any reference to you holding a Back Country Fishing Licence as required by law to be able to fish the Wilkin River. We note that several 24-hour licences have been purchased in your name but these alone do not allow for fishing in designated Backcountry waters such as the Wilkin, Dingle and Young rivers. A whole season licence is required to obtain the Back Country Fishery Licence endorsement. Fishing without a Back-country Licence is an offence which carries a maximum penalty of NZ$5000.00. . . . This is now a compliance investigation which could lead to a Court prosecution being taken in your name.

Whoa! This seemed dire. But it just so happened that I had a copy of my back country license handy as a PDF file, a file that New Zealand Fish & Game had delivered to my inbox after I entered the code from one of the 24-hour licenses I'd purchased, as I'd been instructed to do. I sent my new pen pal a copy of the backcountry license and brief note explaining how I'd acted in good faith, it was just a glitch in the website code and some poorly crafted instructions, no hard feelings on my part. The next missive from Otago did not strike quite the conciliatory tone I had hoped for:

The web pages where the backcountry licence is issued is very clear about the need for a whole season licence. I note that you selected the 'Non Resident Whole Season' as a licence type which should have rung some alarm bells as well. (That's actually providing false information—potentially an additional offence.)

Thus began an extended cross-hemisphere correspondence, me alternately pleading, pugilistic, and evasive as I tried to buy time while working the back channels with my contacts at the New Zealand Fish & Game public relations office. My nemesis proved steadfast, resolute, unmoved by neither emotion, reason, nor any interest in preserving now-imperiled United States–New Zealand relations. My PR contact's hands were tied.

With the payment deadline approaching (and the "court prosecution in my name" looming menacingly in the shadows), I called a pleasant clerk in Dunedin and gave her my credit card information, authorizing a charge of NZ$500.

A few weeks later, I received a check from *The Washington Post*. US$500.

With current exchange rates, I'm still ahead by $100 and change.

Smallmouth in Greater Portland

I CUT MY TEETH ON FLY FISHING BY CASTING POPPERS TO SMALLMOUTH bass during summer visits to my grandparents in Maine. They were great fun—usually willing, often leaping, and never very far away. And they helped illustrate the occasional advantages of the fly rod over conventional tackle; I could place my popper back into the lily pads the fish preferred much faster than my friend and his Abu-Garcia.

When I arrived in Oregon 16 years ago, I didn't have smallmouth on my mind. Like most Portland-area anglers, my sights were set toward the Deschutes, the Wilson, and the Metolius among the region's many salmonid strongholds. But the smallies were here. And I'd never taken notice.

"Smallmouth bass have been in the Columbia and Lower Willamette since the 1930s," said Gary Galovich, a warm-water fish biologist with the Oregon Department of Fish and Wildlife. "We have well-documented reports of a release of smallmouth in Lake Oswego in the early '20s, and another in the Yakima River around the same time. People who came west brought their favorite fisheries along. It didn't take long for the smallmouth to expand their range." Bronzebacks range from estuarial waters to the Idaho border, and have infiltrated most tributaries. The warmer, slower water of the dammed Columbia has been a boon for smallies. In the pools between Bonneville, The Dalles, and John Day dams, fish average one to two and a half pounds, with fish to four pounds a regular occurrence. (The state record fish in both Washington and Oregon hover just below nine pounds.)

The presence of several tournaments on the Columbia and the Willamette are testament to the fishery's staying power. Though this is not good news for everyone. Bass are voracious predators, and as they mature, small fish can make up a significant portion of their diet. Salmonid fry and parr are on the menu. "The impact smallmouth have on salmon and steelhead in the Columbia is unclear," Galovich continued, "though there's no doubt they do eat salmonids. Given habitat preferences, there is some separation between salmonids and bass. That being said, there's also overlap." (On a positive note, smallmouth do eat juvenile northern pike minnow, which may pose an even greater threat to young salmonids.)

Thanks to warming river temps, smallmouth are penetrating further and further into traditional Columbia Basin salmonid habitat. A 2014 snorkel survey by University of Washington biologists recently showed that smallmouth are successfully spawning at river mile 68 on the North Fork John Day River, 22 miles upstream from where bass nests were found in 2010. In response to concerns about salmonid predation, Washington is considering removing limits for bass. The abundance of smallies in the Pacific Northwest stands in sharp contrast to their status on one of the bronzeback's endemic strongholds, Pennsylvania's Susquehanna River. Here, many fish have been developing open sores and lesions, and mature males have female eggs in their testes and other female characteristics. Susquehanna regulars fear the fishery is in steep decline.

A Thursday morning in May, Shane Blitch turned off McLoughlin Boulevard into the Milwaukie Riverfront Park, less than 15 minutes from downtown Portland. There's a bank and movie theater across the street; before us, the lake-like waters of the Willamette. Soon we were gliding in Shane's canoe toward the mouth of Johnson Creek, a few hundred yards north.

"There are number of places on the Willamette I chase smallies," Shane, a potter by trade, said as he paddled. "This town spot is perfect for a quick fix. There are five good spots, and I've caught fish to six pounds in each of them. The big fish are only in the shallower water in May and early June. But you can catch 8-inch to 12-inch fish all summer."

At Johnson Creek, I cast to submerged logs and other "structure," recalling Jimmy Houston's advice from the outdoor programs of my youth. A group of five teenage truants were huddled on the left bank. Had I had a pack of cigarettes or a few PBR tallboys to offer, I could've been their god. I didn't, so instead cast one of Shane's crawdad patterns in their direction. There were no takers this morning, but I did mistake a sea lion for a floating log until it sounded. "It's usually on or it's not," Shane said as we loaded up the canoe. "I'll get nothing for two outings, then it's red hot on the third." A salmon guide with one of the biggest jetboats I'd ever seen launched as we were taking off. Our canoe and fly rods must have seemed effete at best.

Should trends continue, he might be one day fishing for smallies too.

About the Author

Chris Santella is a freelance writer and marketing communications consultant based in Portland, Oregon. He is the author of nineteen books, including the "Fifty Places" series from Stewart, Tabori & Chang/Abrams. His titles include:

- *Fifty Places to Fly Fish Before You Die*
- *Fifty Places to Play Golf Before You Die*
- *Fifty Places to Sail Before You Die*
- *Fifty Places to Go Birding Before You Die*
- *Fifty Places to Dive Before You Die*
- *Fifty MORE Places to Play Golf Before You Die*
- *Fifty Places to Hike Before You Die*
- *Fifty MORE Places to Fly Fish Before You Die*
- *Fifty Places to Bike Before You Die*
- *Fifty Places to Ski and Snowboard Before You Die*
- *Fifty Places to Paddle Before You Die*
- *Fifty Places to Camp Before You Die*
- *Fifty Places to Drink Beer Before You Die*
- *Fifty Favorite Fly Fishing Tales*
- *The Hatch Is On (Globe Pequot)*
- *Once In A Lifetime Trips (Clarkson Potter)*
- *Why I Fly Fish (Abrams)*
- *Cat Wars: The Devastating Consequences of a Cuddly Killer (with Dr. Peter Marra)*

Chris has more than 600,000 hardcover books in print. In addition to his book writing, he is a regular contributor to the *New York Times*, *The Washington Post*, *Fly Rod & Reel*, and *Trout*, and has also contributed to *The New Yorker*, *Robb Report*, *Travel & Leisure*, *The Wall Street Journal*, and *Links*, among other publications. His two "Fifty Places" fly fishing books were adapted for television by the World Fishing Network as *Fifty Places to Fly Fish Before You Die*, which premiered in 2015.